BACKROADS & BYWAYS OF
OREGON

A serene country road not far from Portland. LAURA STANFILL

BACKROADS & BYWAYS OF
OREGON

Drives, Daytrips
& Weekend Excursions

Crystal Wood

The Countryman Press
Woodstock, Vermont

Backroads & Byways of Oregon
ISBN: 978-0-88150-835-2

Interior photographs by the author unless otherwise specified
Map by Paul Woodward, © The Countryman Press
Book design by Hespenheide Design
Composition by Eugenie Delaney

Published by The Countryman Press, P.O. Box 748, Woodstock, VT 05091

Distributed by W. W. Norton & Company, Inc., 500 Fifth Avenue, New York, NY 10110

Printed in the United States of America

10 9 8 7 6 5 4 3 2 1

Thanks to my traveling companions:
Allison, Ricky, Kim, Laura, and Hadley.
Thank you also to the generous J.T.
And thanks to the Oregonians who shared
their favorite spots, historical interests,
and love of Oregon.

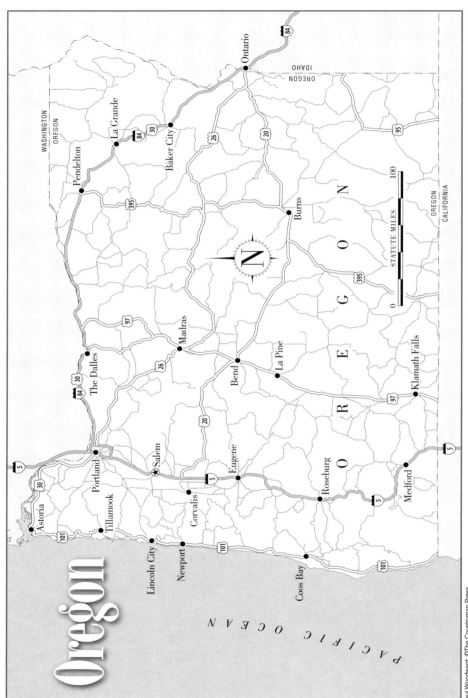

Oregon

PACIFIC OCEAN

Contents

The Coquille Broiler offers local gossip, along with a tasty lunch.

Introduction

We go westward as into the future, with a spirit of enterprise and adventure.
                              —HENRY DAVID THOREAU

Oregon, the seventh largest state in the lower 48, welcomes you! It seems a lot of people haven't yet discovered what's so phenomenal about Oregon. But once you've driven to different points throughout the state, you'll wonder why you didn't visit sooner and how soon you can come back to see all that you couldn't cover in just one trip. Before you start your Oregon adventures, a little familiarity with the state can only help to make your visit a more satisfying one.

Many states have name pronunciation issues. Oregon is no different. If you can get some of the major names correct, you'll get fewer winces from proud Oregonians along the way. But most importantly, the third syllable in "Oregon" is not pronounced "gawn" or "gone." There may be a bit of debate on the rest of the name but beyond any doubt, the last syllable is pronounced "gun." In this book there are hints on regional pronunciation, but if your destination isn't listed ask a local. Oregonians are a very nice bunch.

The "Don't like the weather here, wait 10 minutes" joke is popular in Oregon, as it is in other states. In western Oregon, especially the rain-saturated parts, they like this one: "What follows five days of sunshine? Satur-

Rich soil and copious rain produce stellar fruits and vegetables. LAURA STANFILL

day and Sunday!" But after you've driven through the state, you'll find that the famous rain does not permeate the state, not by a long shot. The best thing to do is dress in layers, no matter the season or the location.

All the trips in this book are made on roads that any sedan can handle. This was done with purpose: Drivers—visitors and residents—have become lost or stranded due to taking a shortcut or feeling their car could handle the weather or terrain. It is always recommended that you check on the roads and highways before you leave. Even in early summer, snow can still close some roads. Your best bet is the Oregon Department of Transportation's TripCheck, (1-800-977-6368 or 511; www.trip check.com). Their continuous updates, road cameras, and construction details will help you get to your destination in a timely and safe manner. Cell phone coverage can be spotty around the state. It's best to check with TripCheck before getting on the road, as well as from the road. Also, pack your car with water, food, a blanket, and a tire inflator/sealant.

Depending on where in the state you plan on visiting and for how long, you may want to consider prepurchasing regional passes or passports. The Pacific Coast Passport covers entrance, day-use fee, and parking at all 16 state/federal fee sites along the entire Oregon coast. From Fort Stevens State Park near Astoria to Shore Acres State Park outside of Coos Bay, many of the parks mentioned in this book are included in the passport. Passports may be purchased at all Forest Service and Oregon Parks and Recreation offices along the Oregon coast. Currently, the five-day pass is a real bargain at only $10. The National Forest Recreation Pass is convenient because unvalidated days are bought in advance and then validat-

Mother and baby alpaca enjoying the sun.   LAURA STANFILL

ed by the purchaser on the days they're needed. This pass can be purchased at www.discovernw.org or by calling 1-800-270-7504. A statewide list of local vendors can be found at www.fs.fed.us.

If you'd like to show your appreciation for the beauty and splendor throughout the state, it's easy to do. When you're hiking at Hells Canyon or searching for agates at Whiskey Run Beach, you may come upon some trash left behind by others, brought in with the high tide or blown in from parts unknown. Place it in a bag and dispose of it properly; that will be thanks enough.

Oregon's Fun Facts

It is unlawful for you to pump your own gas in Oregon. The only exceptions are gas stations on sovereign land and it is the tribe's choice. The only other state in the union with a similar law is New Jersey.

Oregon's lyrical motto is Alis Volat Propriis. Translation: She Flies with Her Own Wings.

Oregon has 50 covered bridges, the most for any state west of the Mississippi and one of the largest totals in the nation. For a detailed guide, including driving directions, visit www.oregon.gov/odot/hwy /bridge.

The state's provocative history can be found around every bend.

The Oregon coast, from the water to up to 16 vertical feet above the low tide mark, is under public ownership, thanks to the Oregon Beach Bill of 1967. This legislation was partially achieved in 1913 by the state legislature's declaring the entire shore a state highway.

The nation's first Bottle Bill—requiring deposits on cans and bottles of soda and beer—was passed in Oregon in 1971.

Oregon enacted prohibition of liquor three years before the national version. All packaged and distilled spirits are owned and sold by the Oregon Liquor Control Commission. All 242 liquor stores here are state operated.

Oregon has more ghost towns than any other state.

As of 2008, there are 395 wineries here (third highest number in the nation), equaling 20,000 planted acres, 11,200 of which are pinot noir grapes.

The last tsunami to strike the Oregon coast was in 1964, caused by a magnitude 9.2 earthquake off the coast of Alaska.

Statewide, there are 6,150 lakes and 111,619 miles of rivers and streams.

What most know as hazelnuts are technically filberts. Whatever you call them, they're the official state nut and most of the world's supply is grown in Oregon.

There are 13 Big Tree National Champions in Oregon. These are recorded as the largest specimens of their type in the country.

In 2009, there were 117 farmers' markets throughout the state and the list is still growing.

The surprisingly posh Geiser Grand Hotel in Baker City. COURTESY GEISER GRAND HOTEL

A marionberry is a variety of blackberry developed in 1945 to suit western Oregon's climate. It has been proposed that it be Oregon's official state berry.

The state's coastline is chock-full of secret spots. LAURA STANFILL

The best way to enjoy Oregon is to get off Interstates 5 and 84. You can't get to know anyplace by whizzing by it on the freeway at breakneck speed. It's like saying you've been to some destination simply because you've had a layover at the airport. Where's the adventure in that?

The Caples House Museum in Columbia City.

CHAPTER

1

Lewis and Clark's Highway

Portland to Astoria

Estimated length: 90 miles
Estimated time: 5 hours to drive straight through and back, or up to 3 full days.

Getting There: OR 30 leads directly out of northwest Portland and follows the Columbia River west to Astoria, where the mouth of the mighty Columbia River meets the Pacific Ocean.

Highlights: There was a time when OR 30 was not only the busiest road to the coast but the most difficult to drive, too. In decades past, it could take half a day. To Oregon writer Ralph Friedman it was "like trying to follow the outlines of a pretzel in a murky basin after the lights were turned off." Luckily the road is much improved since he wrote that apt description. No matter what the road used to be like, it was never as hard a journey as Lewis and Clark's—their "highway" was mostly the Columbia River. Any road that ends at Astoria, the oldest American settlement west of the Rockies, is well worth the time it takes to get there. And from Portland, it's almost no time at all.

Just before you leave Portland metro, you'll be passing two swell spots, and since you're in the Portland area, it would be a shame not to mention

The little antiques stores on the side of the highway may hold just the treasure you've been searching for.

them. To your left, you'll notice acres and acres of forested land fittingly named **Forest Park.** Lewis and Clark paddled up the Willamette River far enough to see what is now Forest Park. Their journals talk about Douglas firs with trunks 5 to 8 feet wide. Although efforts to preserve this area as a park started in 1909 with a 52-acre donation to the city, the idea really got momentum in 1947, when top civic leaders were able to secure 4,200 more acres. The park is now about 5,100 acres and is the largest forested natural area within city limits in the United States. The park contains more than 70 miles of trails, including the Wildwood Trail. This trail is 30 miles long and is part of the **40 Mile Loop,** a system that connects southwest Portland to Gresham in the east via trails and pedestrian walkways. This longer loop does require leaving the pretty spots a few times, but that is being worked on. Eventually, it will link up to another trail that will take hikers and bikers beyond the town of Boring. Further in the future, the trail will end at the Mount Hood area, meeting up with the beloved Pacific Crest Trail.

To your right at almost the same point is **St. John's Bridge.** This is the tallest bridge in Portland and undoubtedly its most attractive. No matter the weather, the bridge's 440-foot-high gothic towers are a sight to behold. When the fog and drizzle of winter move in, it looks like a scene from a Henry James novel. Construction started a month after the stock market crash of the Great Depression and was completed in 21 months, 1 million dollars under budget. It was the first bridge to require aviation lights on the towers.

The first stop comes just minutes after leaving Portland. It's a bit of paradise right outside city limits, called **Sauvie Island** (pronounced *saw-vee*). Depending on the season, there may be a corn maze and pumpkin patches or hiking and bird-watching. Whenever you visit, it's always lovely. Lewis and Clark made it here in 1805, calling the island "Wap-pa-to" or "Wa-pa-too" for the edible root plant that grew wild here. This hearty plant, plus the wealth of game and waterfowl, made the island a summer and fall home for the Multnomah Indians, as well pioneers and settlers. Like many spots around North America, the island was later renamed after a Hudson's Bay Company employee.

Although it only happens June through August, the smallest working farm on the island, **Sauvie Island Lavender Farm,** holds an informal lavender tea service. It comes with lavender tea or lavender lemonade and fresh baked lavender-lemon shortbread. The farm also has lavender wand–

making classes and u-pick yellow plums and mulberries. If you're here in the fall, then the **Pumpkin Patch** will provide classic fun. Their corn maze is cut into a different, detailed "picture" every year. The **Sauvie Island Wildlife Area** is 12,000- plus acres, open mid-April through September. Parking permits can be bought at Sam's Market at the foot of the bridge and at other stores on the island. Hiking and bird-watching can be fruitful, with 250 species, including bald eagles, stopping here. October through November is the peak season for many birds. The eagles, however, hang around from December to March looking for prey. **Howell Territorial Park** is a peaceful 93-acre park with a pioneer-era orchard and herb garden. On premises is the Bybee-Howell House, an 1850s farmhouse not open for tours at the time of this writing but which still makes a lovely picnic backdrop. During summer and early fall, a pleasant 2.5-mile trail loops around a peninsula called **Oak Island.** Once at the heart of this island, you'll be surrounded by water on three sides. There are beaches for the public to enjoy. Please note that after October 1, the area is open to hunters. Off Reeder Road is Walton Beach, which is very family friendly, but you may find garbage strewn about. A little farther north is the infamous clothing-optional Collins Beach. You've been notified . . . At the end of Reeder Road, a mile after the pavement ends, you'll find a parking lot and the beginning of a 3-mile trail to **Warrior Rock Lighthouse.** Abandoned now, it was built in 1889 and had the oldest fog bell in the Pacific Northwest. The bell now sits at the county's historic courthouse in Saint Helens. It's not a large lighthouse like the beauties along the Oregon coast, but the trail is a nice hike all the same.

Named after a view of that loud mountain 39 miles away, Saint Helens at one time had the primary deep-water port, used even more than Portland's. But after it was twice destroyed by suspicious fires, that left Portland to claim the honor. If you're passing through at mealtime, stop at the **Klondike Restaurant and Bar**, which features steaks. If just a nosh is needed, the **Houlton Bakery** makes its products, from baked goods to sandwiches and pizza, fresh. This is why what's available on any given day changes often. Just be flexible and you'll be satisfied. Fans of the movie *Twilight* will want to see Charlie's house. It's a private residence so please enjoy it from the street. At **Jilly's** you can peruse capes, prom dresses, and purple fairy wings just like those worn in the movie. The owner has such an interesting and eclectic mix of clothing and accessories that her items were used in the film and purchased by the cast and crew for personal use.

Along the Columbia River are plenty of spots for watching the boats glide by.

In Columbia City is the **Caples House Museum.** Once the home of the county's first physician it, along with the tool shed and carriage house, has been restored into a museum by the Daughters of the American Revolution. On the grounds are a small country gift shop and apple trees. When the apples are ripe, the little orchard becomes a u-pick. Behind the Caples

House is **Pixie Park,** a quiet spot with easy access to sit and watch the traffic on the Columbia River drift silently by.

Near the town of Prescott and before Rainier is an unusual place to play disc golf. That's because this was the land on which the Trojan Nuclear Power Plant once stood. The plant was in closed in 1993, then, in 2006, the cooling tower was imploded. The area is now known as the **Trojan PGE Park.** Visitors can also fish, hike, and bird watch, as well as play an 18-hole disc-golf course. Because Portland is the hometown of *The Simpsons'* creator, Matt Groening, it's been speculated that the Springfield Power Plant (where Homer works) was based upon the now-defunct plant. When Lewis and Clark came through the area, Clark complained in his writings, "I slept very little for the noise kept during the whole night by the swans, geese, white and great Brant ducks, etc."

As you pass through Rainier, the cantilever bridge to your right is the **Lewis and Clark Bridge**. At the time of its construction it was the longest and highest of its type in the country. It was designed by Joseph Baermann Strauss who was also chief engineer of the design of the Golden Gate Bridge. Once you are past the bridge, you will find two overlooks. The first fills up easily. Instead, stay on the highway and go past it to the second overlook, which tends to be less crowded; it is just as amazing. If it's daytime, pull over and take full advantage of its views of Mounts Rainier, Saint Helens, Hood, and Adams, and of course the Columbia River, make this a must-stop.

The **Flippin Castle** is a cheeky name but Thomas Flippin was very serious about a man's home being his castle, even though he and his wife only lived in it for three years before separating. The house was pretty elaborate for the area and is now owned by the Clatskanie Senior Citizens. There's a tour of the house; lunch can be had in its cafeteria for a very nominal fee. Clatskanie's historic business district is a pleasant walk among original buildings. And keep an eye out for a distinctive dimensional woodcarving commemorating the 200th anniversary of the Lewis and Clark Expedition.

The berries grown throughout Oregon are world famous. Once you have them fresh picked, those available at the local grocery store may pale in comparison. To help get you through your berry cravings once you return home, stop by the **Berry Patch** restaurant in Westport. There you'll find syrups, jams, jellies, and pie filling made with local loganberries, marionberries, raspberries, boysenberries, huckleberries, and strawberries.

Bradley Oregon State Wayside has views of Columbia and in 1922 was one of the first of parcels of land to be donated to the Oregon Highway Commission. It offers public restrooms, picnic tables, and a nice view of the Columbia.

At the **Twilight Eagle Sanctuary** a viewing platform looks over marshes and islands. It's great for observing birds and other wildlife, with interpretive panels about the eagles and other birds, as well as Lewis and Clark's journey at this point. If these don't interest you, then there's no other reason to stop here.

You've no doubt heard about Oregon's rain. And as you drive around the state, you will notice this can't be true for the entire state, and it isn't. Not even close. But here in **Astoria,** the legendary rain is serious business. As serious as 75 inches a year. This is not a misprint. In Portland, the yearly average is about 37 inches. And keep in mind that most of those 75 inches are likely to happen between late October and late May. The winter that Lewis and Clark stayed in the area, it rained all but 12 days. Maybe this is why the population of Astoria has grown by less than 1,500 in the last 100 years.

If the rain didn't make the settlers, loggers, fur trappers, and fisherman of Astoria tough, then the work surely did. The Columbia River is a highly valued waterway for ships to go 100 miles inland. It's busy and dangerous. There have been over 200 major shipwrecks in this "graveyard of the Pacific."

With its hills filled with Victorian homes, the longest three-span truss bridge in the world, and its location where the Columbia and the Pacific meet, Astoria is impressive. But to really gain a scope on this notable town of just 10,000, you have to head up to the **Astoria Column.** The column stands 164 steps high and has an observation deck at the top. It's an awful lot of stairs and narrow at that, but well worth the climb once the top is reached. Before heading up, purchase a slight balsa-wood glider to toss from the top. The money goes to help pay for the recent renovations, as well as upkeep of the column. If scaling those stairs seems daunting, the view without going inside the column is still spectacular. There's also a burial canoe memorial to Chief Concomly, a Chinook chief known for friendly relations with European and American explorers. His grandson went on to become the first man to teach English in Japan (to 14 samurais, no less) and later was a chief interpreter for Commodore Perry.

If you want know how a sea captain/millionaire lived in the mid-1880s,

You can climb to the top of the Astoria Column or admire it from below. BEN WAISANEN

you'd better visit the **Flavel House Museum.** As Astoria's first millionaire, George Flavel had the most elaborate of all the area's homes at the time. This 1885 Queen Anne has been furnished with Victorian pieces. At over 11,500 square feet, it's gigantic, with six unique fireplace mantels and 14- and 12-foot-high ceilings. More than once it was thought that the home was too expensive to restore and upkeep, and therefore should be torn down. Each time, residents and civic leaders stepped forward to see about other options.

Before CGI (computer-generated imagery) took over filmmaking, shooting on location was pivotal. And because Astoria looks like a town out of the movies, it only makes sense that some beloved ones were filmed here, in particular, *The Goonies.* Some spots to check out: The Goonies' house is found at 368 38th Street. Park on the street and be respectful, as this is a private residence. The jailhouse in the opening scenes is found at the corner of Seventh and Duane. Sorry, Fratellis' restaurant was just a façade and torn down after the film had wrapped. You can also visit locations from *Kindergarten Cop, Short Circuit, Free Willy, Into the Wild,* and *The Ring 2.* A tour book on all of the film sites in Astoria can be picked up at the Astoria-Warrenton Chamber of Commerce.

Entertainment in Astoria is like that found elsewhere around the state: plentiful and talented. At the **Astor Street Opry Company,** audiences are treated to fun entertainment, often very family friendly. They've been putting on a locally written melodrama, *Shangaied in Astoria,* for decades. It's a rip-roaring good time complete with opportunities to boo and cheer.

This show usually runs for most the summer, and for one week it goes "topsey turvey," when the women and men play one another's roles, all in the name of fundraising. The group also puts on other shows throughout the year. At the **Liberty Theater** is a selection of plays, concerts, musicals, film festivals, and other live entertainment. The building itself can't help but be noticed as you walk by. The bygone era it comes from has been lovingly and elegantly restored. Consider seeing a performance you might not normally attend, just to get inside to look at the chandeliers, ornate wall carvings, and diverse paint colors.

Not every kid in this country has to have the same toys from the same megastores. Sometimes it's good to get them something a little bit different. Just don't tell them it's "educational." **Purple Cow Toys** carries these not-everyday toys, as well as many classics thought to have become extinct in today's too-technological world. There are some items here that adults who don't take themselves too seriously might like, too.

A true souvenir is something that is much easier to acquire in the locale it comes from than anywhere else. **Shallon Winery** offers wines made from

While in Astoria, check out what's happening at the stunning Liberty Theater.

whey or fruit and even one made from chocolate. Before you turn up your trained nose, go in and have a taste. **Gimre's** has been outfitting feet since 1892, making it the oldest shoe store west of the Rockies. You'll be doing a lot of walking here in Astoria; if you're worried because your shoe size is a bit unusual, this store will have you covered.

Astoria has some really great lodging options, from the posh and historic to the quaint and comfortable. The first question to ask is, is sleeping late in the morning important? If so, and you're inflexible about this, stay away from hotels on the Columbia River. This tumultuous water highway starts getting busy at the crack of dawn. And though there are no car horns, you would hear an erratic symphony of ship and boat horns. To some this is romantic and a delightful way to start the morning. To others, this is a vacation and there shouldn't be a jolting alarm clock of any shape, size, or sound.

Getting a room on the water is one thing, but getting a luxury suite so close to the ships coming through that the pilots themselves stay there is the ultimate. At the **Astoria Pilot House** you have 180-degree views of the Columbia River and all the traffic upon it. You also have three bedrooms and bath, a full kitchen, a formal dining room and, should you need it, a private dock. This is the spot where the ships would change pilots, from river to sea or vice versa. Often the water is too rough and dangerous to bring the ship in and so the pilots need to have two different set of skills. One was to live here and ferry back and forth to their awaiting ship. **Holiday Inn Express** is a surprisingly good spot to stay. While obviously the name is well known, you may be tempted to shy away for the same reason. But it is well appointed and clean, with an amiable staff. Although sadly there aren't balconies, you will still be on the water: the same river that some other hotels will charge more for.

For a smallish town, there are a slew of dining options in Astoria. It's usually best to eat where the locals do, and the pancakes and enormous omelets at **Andrew & Steve's Café** hold you to that truth. It's not fancy, it's not themed, and it's not picture-pretty, but its fare is reliably delicious, with warm service. The restaurant has been operated by three generations of the same family since 1916, even through Astoria's great fire. If you're just a coffee person, head to **Flying Barney's Rusty Cup and Beanery.** This small storefront carries a few baked items but really it's about the coffee. Live through rainy winters like these folks and you'll understand why the coffee craze started in the Pacific Northwest.

Oregon is known throughout the world for its microbreweries and Astoria is no exception. **Fort George Brewery and Public House** is located in what was the town's first car dealership; now instead of a Model Ts waiting behind the windows, it's a brewery. One of its two public restrooms uses car parts in the decorations. For some reason, the other is decorated with a jungle theme. Eight house beers are served here, plus one seasonal. There is also the popular Guest Beer, which could be from around Oregon or the world. Whichever it is, it won't be one that can be easily picked up at the market. With 10 to 12 beers to choose from, there should be something for all microbrew lovers. The menu offers a variety of items from rockfish tacos to house-made sausages. And as this is a spot for locals as well as visitors, it can get pretty busy. And though the service is friendly, it can be a bit inefficient. But a good attitude goes a long way and the employees have that. Those under 21 are welcome until 9 PM. At **Clemente's** you can support multiple causes in one appetizing meal—organic items, local and sustainable foods, environmentally minded, exposure to new artists. Although this wouldn't be considered a budget eatery, the prices are very reasonable for the quality of food, especially for seafood. And the fixed-price menu available at dinner is well within range. The food here takes time. Oysters aren't shucked until you order them, and so on. Dine elsewhere if on a time limit. Every three months, works from a different local artist are displayed. As at a gallery, the restaurant's décor is subtle and leaves the rest to the art. The lounge offers tidbits of the restaurant's menu but on low couches and, on the right nights, with live jazz.

In a town steeped in its resplendent past, it makes sense that there are hotels paying homage to it. From the boutique-size lobby at the **Hotel Elliott** to its art deco rooms, the design elements of the past are the center of attention instead of competing with overly ornate décor. Originally opened in 1924, the hotel underwent a three-year renovation and reopened in 2003. The suites are snuggly instead of overblown and ostentatious, yet the bathrooms' stone floor is heated. The hotel demonstrates how the relationship between then and now can work best. The site for **Cannery Pier Hotel** was exactly that, a cannery. The pilings of the onetime fisherman-owned cannery the hotel sits on are over 100 years old. Now it's a posh place in which to listen to the ship horns, enjoy wine, and check out a Finnish spa. At 600 feet into the Columbia River, the rooms' balconies are very becoming. Although the hotel isn't historic, the architecture is made to look so. If you're tired of driving but need a lift to downtown, ask for a

The Hotel Elliott has been completely remodeled and yet retains its historic architecture.   KIMBERLY PHILLIPPE

complimentary chauffeured ride in the hotel's 1939 Buick Special. That's one sweet ride.

There's so much more to do in Astoria. It's remarkable that a place so relaxing can keep visitors so busy. There's the **Columbia River Maritime Museum** with its mind-bending display of a Coast Guard rescue ship (coastal residents have a particular high regard for this vital service branch). Here you can tour the Lightship Columbia and learn about how invaluable bar pilots are. If you think maritime history is boring, then a trip here is absolutely required. You also visit the **Uppertown Firefighters Museum**, which houses firefighting equipment from 1873 to 1963, and the living history demonstrations at **Fort Clatsop National Memorial**.

Astoria's pedestrian-friendly and aesthetic downtown is full of dining and shopping choices. When you're tired of walking, the **Astoria Trolley** runs along most of the historic riverfront in a refurbished 1913 trolley. The staff is comprised of bighearted volunteers who know a thing or two about the town's history and are generous with their anecdotes. A round trip takes about an hour and is extremely well priced. In Astoria over 350 homes still in use are over 100 years old. Drive up into the hills south of downtown, find a good parking spot, and walk through the neighborhoods.

And as if Astoria didn't have enough to do, you can continue on over the bridge into Warrenton. At Fort Stevens you'll find the only U.S. mainland site shelled in World War II, two swimming spots at Coffenbury Lake, an interesting military museum, and a deck to view the beached remains of the shipwreck of the 1906 *Peter Iredale.* September though October is mushroom-hunting season. Ranger-guided mushroom walks can be found on most Friday and Saturdays during these months. Or a very informative brochure and map can be found at the park offices and at www.oregonstateparks.org.

There's so much to do on this trip that if you're bored, it's by choice.

IN THE AREA

Accommodations

Astoria Pilot House, 14th Street and the Columbia River, Astoria. Call 503-289-9926 or 1-888-683-7987. A three-bedroom luxury suite with full kitchen and astounding views. Web site: www.astoriapilothouse.com.

Cannery Pier Hotel, 10 Basin Street, Astoria. Call 503-325-4996 or 1-888-325-4996. Web site: www.cannerypierhotel.com.

Clatskanie River Inn, 600 East Columbia River Highway, Clatskanie. Call 503-728-9000. Newly built hotel with indoor pool. Web site: www .clatskanie.com/riverinn.

Holiday Inn Express, 204 West Marine Drive, Astoria. Call 503-325-6222 or 1-888-898-6222. A good deal for on-the-water lodging. Web site: www.astoriahie.com.

Hotel Elliott, 357 12th Street, Astoria. Call 503-325-2222. Web site: www.hotelelliott.com.

Hudson Parcher Park, 75503 Larson Road, Rainier. Call 503-366-3984.

RV and tent sites. Reservations not taken after noon on Thurs. For the immediate weekend, it's first come, first serve. Web site: www.co .columbia.or.us/parks.

Island Cove Park, 31421 NW Reeder Road. Call 503-621-9701. RV, tent sites, and yurts. Open year-round. Web site: www.islandcovepark.com.

Reeder Beach RV Park, 26048 NW Reeder Road, Sauvie Island. Call 503-621-3970. Open year-round and overlooks the Columbia River. Web site: www.reederbeachrv.com.

Rosebriar Inn, 636 14th Street, Astoria. Call 503-325-7427 or 1-800-487-0224. A bed & breakfast in a 1920s building with 12 rooms and private baths. Web site: www.rosebriar.net.

Scappoose Creek Inn, 53758 West Lane Road, Scappoose. Historic farmhouse bed & breakfast. Each room has its own bathroom and includes breakfast. Call 503-543-2740. Web site: www.scappoosecreek inn.com.

Scappoose RV Park, 34036 North Honeyman Road, Scappoose.

Attractions and Recreation

Astor Street Opry Company, 129 West Bond Street, Uniontown, Astoria. Call 503-325-6104. Web site: www.astorstreetoprycompany.com.

Astoria Column, top of Coxcumb Hill, Astoria. Call 503-325-2963. Climb 164 steps up to an observation deck and unparalleled view. Open from dawn to dusk.

Astoria Guitar Company, 399 31st Street, Astoria. Vintage and new guitars. Call 503-298-0340.

Astoria Regatta, Astoria. Call 503-325-6311. The oldest festival in the Northwest happens each mid-Aug. Web site: www.astoriaregatta.org.

Astoria Riverfront Trolley. Catch it anywhere on the riverfront between Basin and 39th. Wave your dollar so the operator knows to stop and not just wave back. Operating Memorial Day to Labor Day, noon to 7 PM.

Blue Heron Herbary, 27731 NW Reeder Road, Sauvie Island. Call 503-621-1457. The garden has over 300 varieties of herbs and is sectioned into Asian, Mediterranean, Tea, Medicinal, Shakespearean, and more. Open Mar. until Nov., then Thanksgiving to Christmas.

Bowpicker, 17th and Duane streets, Astoria. Look for the boat-shaped food cart serving the best fish and chips on the Oregon coast.

Columbia River Maritime Museum, 1792 Marine Drive, Astoria. Call 503-325-2323. Open daily. Web site: www.crmm.org.

Dinosaurs Unlimited Scenic Tours and Aerobatic Flights. Fly in a 1942 Stearman biplane. Call 503-939-0252.

Fernhill Glass, 92884 Fern Hill Road, Astoria. Call 503-325-3448. Hand-blown glass floats, ornaments, and decorative items. Web site: www.fern hillglass.com.

You can't not learn something at the Columbia River Maritime Museum.
KIMBERLY PHILLIPPE

Finnware, 1116 Commercial Street, Astoria. Call 503-325-5720. If it's Scandinavian, there's a good chance you'll find it here.

Flavel House Museum, 441 Eighth Street, Astoria. Call 503-325-2203. Tour the house of Captain Flavel, Astoria's first millionaire. Web site: www.cumtux.org.

The Flippin Castle, 620 SW Tichenor Street, Clatskanie. Call 503-728-3608. Tour a home built in the 1900s and stay for lunch in the Senior Center cafeteria. Web site: www.clatskaniecastle.com.

Gimre's, 239 14th Street, Astoria. Call 503-325-3972 or 1-888-622-6130. Carries a wide selection of hard-to-find shoe sizes. Web site: www.gimres shoes.com.

Heritage Museum, 1618 Exchange Street, Astoria. Call 503-325-2203. Web site: www.cumtux.org.

Holly McHone Jewelry, 1150 Commercial Street, Astoria. Call 503-325-8029. Custom-designed diamond and colored gemstone jewelry. Web site: www.hollymchone.com.

Jilly's, 299 South First Street, St. Helens. Call 503-397-4083. Shop where the cast and crew of *Twilight* shopped, right down to the purple fairy wings.

Josephson's, 106 Marine Drive, Astoria. Call 503-325-2190. Smoking seafood for four generations. Web site: www.josephsons.com.

Lady Washington, varied ports along the Columbia River, including Astoria. Check schedule for voyage locations. Call 1-800-200-5239. Web site: www.historicalseaport.org.

Liberty Theater, 1203 Commercial Street, Astoria. Call 503-325-5922. Refurbished theater with an array of events and entertainment year-round. Web site: www.liberty-theather.org.

Lucy's Books, 348 12th Street, Astoria. Call 503-325-4210. A locally owned independent bookstore. Web site: www.lucysbooks.net.

The Pumpkin Patch, 16511 NW Gillihan Road, Sauvie Island. Call 503-621-3874. Pumpkins, corn maze, gift shop, café, hayrides, u-pick, market,

1920s working barn. Open June through Oct. Web site: www.portland
maize.com or www.thepumpkinpatch.com.

Purple Cow Toys, 1380 Commercial Street, Astoria. Call 503-325-2996.
A toy store of simple, imaginative, whimsical, and educational toys.

RiverSea Gallery, 1160 Commercial Street, Astoria. Call 503-325-1270.
Original art and fine jewelry in a 4,000-square-foot gallery. Web site:
www.riverseagallery.com.

Sauvie Island Lavender Farm, 20230 NW Sauvie Island Road, Sauvie
Island. Call 503-577-6565. Will ship their dried lavender bouquet anywhere in America. Open May through Oct. Web site: www.sauvieisland
lavenderfarm.com.

Scandinavian Midsummer Festival, Astoria. Call 1-800-875-6807.
Everything from polkas to bonfires for more than 40 years, each mid-
June. Web site: www.astoriascanfest.com.

Shallon Winery, 1598 Duane Street, Astoria. Call 503-325-5978. Unusual fruit and whey wines, and an even more unusual chocolate wine. Web
site: www.shallon.com.

Shanghaied in Astoria, Astoria. Call 503-325-6104. For 20- plus years,
this melodrama with local actors has entertained. Web site: www.shang
haiedinastoria.com.

Trojan PGE Park, 71760 Columbia River Highway, between Prescott
and Rainier. Enjoy disc-golf, bird watching, and hiking near where a
nuclear power plant once stood.

Twilight Eagle Sanctuary, 2.5 miles east of Astoria, Cathlamet Bay.

Uppertown Firefighters Museum, 2968 Marine Drive, Astoria. Call
503-325-2203. Open Wed. through Sat. Web site: www.cumtux.org.

Dining/Drinks

Andrew & Steve's Café, 1196 Marine Drive, Astoria. Call 503-325-5762.
Home-style goodness for breakfast, lunch, and dinner.

Enjoy local and sustainable foods at Clemente's. KIMBERLY PHILLIPPE

The Berry Patch, 49289 Highway 30, Westport. Call 503-455-2250.

Columbia Café, 1114 Marine Drive, Astoria. Call 503-325-2233. They just don't make restaurants like this anymore. Be prepared to wait and be open to sitting at the counter.

Clemente's, 1198 Commercial Street, Astoria. Call 503-325-1067. Fresh seafood, seasonal menu, and a few vegetarian choices. Lunch and dinner. Closed Mon. Web site: www.clementesrestaurant.com.

Crabarnet Room, 357 12th Street, Astoria. Wine, appetizers, and live music in the basement of the Hotel Elliot.

Flying Barney's Rusty Cup, 1213 Commercial Street, Astoria.

Fort George Brewery and Public House, 1483 Duane Street, Astoria. Call 503-523-7468.

Houlton Bakery, 2155 Columbia Boulevard, St. Helens. Call 503-366-2648.

Klondike Restaurant and Bar, 71 Cowlitz Street, St. Helens. Call 503-366-2634. An old-fashioned family steakhouse. Web site: www.klondike restaurant.com.

Mark's on the Channel, 34326 Johnsons Landing Road, Scappoose. Call 503-543-8765. Open Apr. through Sept. Located on the water. Web site: www.marksonthechannel.com.

Urban Café, 1119 Commercial Street, Astoria. Serving generous portions for lunch and dinner. Live entertainment.

Other Contacts

Astoria-Warrenton Area Chamber of Commerce, 111 West Marine Drive, Astoria. Call 503-325-6311 or 1-800-875-6807.

40 Mile Loop, Portland. Maps of the trails are available at www.40mile loop.org.

The dense pine trees seem to protect the road and the traveler.

2

Ocean to Creek to Lake and Back Again

Northern Central Coast

Estimated length: 50 miles
Estimated time: 2 hours driving straight through, or 3 full days

Getting There: From Salem, head west from downtown on OR 22, following the "Coastal Cities" signs. At OR 18, continue west toward Grande Ronde. Once this hits the famed US 101, turn south toward Lincoln City. This trip starts once you are just past the south end of town, then doubles back. South of town is Immonen Road and two great places to shop for pottery and handblown glass. Heading back on US 101 toward town again, you will see OR 229, Siletz Highway, and Kernville/Drift Creek exit on your right. South Drift Creek Road comes up quickly once you are on OR 229. From here, take Forest Road 17 for about 10 miles. After Drift Creek Falls, continue on Forest Road 17 to return to OR 18. Go right (west) to head back to Lincoln City and OR 101, to continue on this trip.

Highlights: On a map, it looks as if this trip should take no time at all, but that is not the case. The meandering road through **Siuslaw National Forest to Drift Creek Falls, Drift Creek Suspension Bridge,** and **Drift Creek Covered Bridge** seems designed for those in no rush. The artists along the coast will be happy to talk with you about their work and that of nearby fellow creative souls. The 1.5-mile hike to the suspension bridge and waterfall can be done at a fast pace or at one that gives to the chance to enjoy the ocean air made even fresher by the trees and fauna that surrounds you. You could rush this experience, but why? From the falls it's back into town, with a drive around Devil's Lake.

When people visualize what they imagine Oregon to be, this expedition likely matches the images in their mind's eye: trees dripping with moss fed by masses of rain, a waterfall cascading to the ground, a covered bridge from years past, artists demonstrating and sharing their skills and knowledge, and a glimpse of the colossal Pacific coast.

Turning your back to the Pacific Ocean can be difficult, but gazing on the **Siletz Bay Wildlife Refuge** lessens the sting. The refuge is located just south of Lincoln City. At the southern end of the refuge, take Immonen Road on the left. Half a mile in, along a forest-lined road, is **Mossy Creek Pottery.** If you're looking for a traditional-looking retail store, you'll drive right past Mossy Creek. This quaint converted cottage sits on six wooded acres. More than 30 years ago it was turned into a hideaway featuring pottery art. Owned by Dan and Susan Wheeler, the store now carries stoneware, raku clay, and porcelain items from over 40 Northwest potters, including Dan's. He's been a potter for over 20 years. Susan's work in fused glass is present as well. There are so many pieces that every available spot is used for display. As you arrive, you'll notice the porch is an additional gallery of outdoor and lawn art.

Just around the next bend is **Alder House,** a glass-blowing studio. Buzz and Anne Williams have been there since 1968. Originally a paint and pencil artist, Buzz took a one-week course in glass blowing and knew it was his calling. Alder House is one of the studios supplying the elusive glass floats hidden on the beach for the Finders Keepers event (see page 47). Of course, if you're in the area when the hunt isn't going on or if you want a guaranteed treasure to take home in the color of your choice, Buzz has plenty available for purchase. Anne's Witch Balls add a feminine touch in the studio. Not too much is known about the balls' origin except that they were first made in the Northeast and were believed to keep witches and evil spirits away. Glass is a remarkable medium and its being thought of as magical doesn't seem unrealistic.

Enjoy your brief visual encounter with the ocean again as you head back the way you came. Just moments north on Highway 101 is the Kernville exit and Drift Creek Road. If you're feeling a bit peckish, be sure

A historical and geological information kiosk on the Siletz River.

to stop by **Barking Dog Farms,** a certified organic farm run by chef David Schaffer. Along stocking up on fruit and other produce perfect for this soul-cleansing trip, you can sip lemonade or herb tea on their deck that has a lovely view of the **Siletz River.** If they have the time, David and/or his wife, Heidi, enjoy sitting and talking with their visitors.

As you leave the farm, start to look for South Drift Creek Road about ¼ mile down. From there, take Forest Road 17 to the left. After about 10 miles, a sign for parking will be on your right. Once you exit your car, you'll know you're in the right place because you will hear the waterfall long before you see it. (Be sure to pack extra shoes that you won't mind getting muddy. The 1.5-mile hike isn't too difficult, but Oregon rain makes globs of mud that you won't want to track into your car.)

Events in Oregon's small coastal towns don't always get much publicity. Once in Lincoln City, tune in to KBCH radio, 1400 AM. This small local station has its finger on the heartbeat of the area. The town's unofficial mayor, DJ Roger Robertson (affectionately called "Double R" by locals) makes sure that you'll know about everything from the Kiwanis Pancake Breakfast at the firehouse, to the high tide times, to where to buy tickets to the Glass Float Ball. And don't worry about attending KBCH-publicized events thrown for residents. Everyone, visitors included, is always invited.

The **Drift Creek Bridge** is 240 feet long and sits 100 feet above the creek. It takes you through the fairy-tale-like forest canopy to a view of the falls cascading 80 feet below. Once you cross the bridge, a short jaunt will lead you behind the waterfall. The water is quite cold and taking a dip in it might not be as refreshing as it is uncomfortable. The view, however, is magnificent. Take a moment to give thanks to Scott Paul, a U.S. Forest Service trail builder and construction foreman who lost his life in a rigging accident while building the bridge. Be prepared to pay a fee for a Northwest Forest Pass.

After the bridge, continue away from the direction you came on Forest Road 17, until you reach OR 18. A right (east) will take you to Salem, a left (west) continues this trip's circular journey. If you are planning on spending more time in Lincoln City or the Oregon coast, the latter is the direction you want to turn.

Just a few miles down the highway is **Otis,** an unincorporated community owned by the Lematta family since 1910. There is no official population for the area as the homes are in the surrounding hills. Otis is a scant 190 acres and consists of the **Otis Café,** the post office, a gas station, a drive-through espresso stand, and an all-purpose building that has served as a flea market and store for bear carvings made from tree stumps. With the exception of the 3 acres occupied by these businesses, the remaining 187 acres are exclusively for timber or agricultural use. Otis's closest brush with fame came when Vivian Lematta put it up for sale in 1999 and the *Today Show* considered doing a feature on the area. There have also been rumors that Arnold Schwarzenegger was once interested in purchasing it, and that Wal-Mart looked into the possibility of erecting a store there. In 2004, Lematta listed the area for sale a second time, for $3,000,000. A pretty

Just about anyone can learn to blow a glass float at the Jennifer Sears Glass Art Studio.

sound investment, considering her grandfather had purchased it for $5,000. She hasn't lived in the area full-time since 1957.

As quirky as the "town" is, it boasts one of the best places to eat in the entire county—for sure, the best breakfast. The **Otis Café** is small, and when the weather is calm, large parties must be accommodated outside. But if you don't mind getting real close to your fellow diners, the home-made molasses bread and Dutch cheese omelets are worth squeezing in for. Consider stopping and getting a loaf of the bread or a homemade pie to go, if there's no time to eat in.

After you've dined your fill, turn right (west) on Highway 18. After just a few minutes' driving (roughly 4 miles), you'll come to the legendary US 101 heading south toward Lincoln City. A left turn on East Devil's Lake Road will be easy to find, as you will see the lake on your left.

Henry David Thoreau wrote, "A lake is the landscape's most beautiful and expressive feature. It is earth's eye; looking into which the beholder measures the depth of his own nature." Thoreau may have been writing about a much bigger lake than this one, but the sentiment is still appropriate. **Devil's Lake** is a scant 3 miles long—less than 1.5 miles across and 22 feet deep at its deepest spot—but it's the best place to enjoy the sun if the coast is foggy. Once the weather west of the cascades heats up (July through September), the beaches of central Oregon have some fogged-in days. Also, the always present coastal wind doesn't make it the ¼-mile-inland lake. It is little wonder that the Lincoln City locals prefer the lake to the beach for picnics, camping, water sports, and just relaxing.

Although diminutive, Devil's Lake has nine kinds of freshwater fish and is a good place to spot loons, grebes, coots, cormorants, blue herons, and the occasional bald eagle. The latter have an active nest east of the lake and can be seen feeding here. If you do go fishing, please be sure to throw back any grass carp you catch. Not that anyone thinks the grass carp are an endangered breed. They're being used in this lake to help control its aquatic vegetation biologically. This type of carp grows a minimum of 10 pounds a year and eats up to three times its own body weight daily. The voracious appetite of these fish has proven pretty effective.

If the water looks inviting and your toes are calling for some freedom, there are six parks on Devil's Lake, three are on the east side of the lake and the others on the west side. Like the lake, **Sand Point** is small. But it offers nice view and its being located on a jetty provides easy access to the water. Next is **Holmes Road.** Here the access to the water is slight, but the view from the picnic tables makes even the last granola bar in your glove compartment taste better. Just before East Devil's Lake Road ends at Highway 101, you'll come to **Devil's Lake State Park.** A ½-mile easy hike rambles through natural forestland. You'd never know how close you are to an outlet mall.

As you continue west on Devil's Lake Road, you'll run back into the main town and Highway 101. Take a peek at **D River,** the shortest river in the world until recently. Starting in 1940, disputers of its title have tried repeatedly to take it away. One Oregon county's chamber of commerce said they had the shortest river and that the D was merely a brook. Despite the naysayers' claim to the Geodetic-Geographic Board in Washington, D.C., the officials agreed to its official low-tide measurement. From there came official signage from the Oregon Department of Transportation and inclusion into the Guinness World Records. Then in 1987, elementary school kids in Great Falls, Montana, pleaded the case for their Roe River as the world's shortest, all the way to newspapers and television programs nationwide. The Roe was measured and given the title. But Lincoln City wouldn't go down without a fight. They had the D River's length measured again, proving they had the shortest river at 120 feet long, give or take 5 feet. Never being shy of publicity, the Guinness officials reopened the case and decided the two communities could share the title.

If you plan to stay the night in the area, stop at the **Jennifer L. Sears Glass Art Studio** before heading to the Siletz Bay Wildlife Refuge. Something about watching glass be blown into art is mesmerizing, therapeutic, and alluring—one of those "I'd like to try that someday" arts. Glass can be cold and hard but, with the help of these artisans, who also provide the materials, it takes on a warm, malleable fluidity. There's no reason to be intimidated here. The instructors are engaging and encouraging. Their knowledge keeps you on the right path to making a glass float, starfish, vase, paperweight, or almost anything else you can think of. Jonathan Myers, one of the managing glass artists, once helped make a bathroom sink for a customer. Visit at just the right time and the studio may have a rare calcedonia which won't be available any other time. Once it's gone, it's gone. Any traveler can buy a souvenir, but this experience enables you to create the item that inspires your vacation memories. Anyone eight years of age or older can make a piece; prices start at $75. Reservations are strongly recommended during the summer months. No time to blow glass? Check out **Volta,** their art gallery located directly across the street, for an already made piece of glass art.

Once the creative learning process starts it can be hard to stop. At the **Pacific Coast Center for Culinary Arts** (CCCA), classes are taught with an emphasis on local ingredients, wine, or cheese. CCCA has a full-time on-staff chef, and area chefs teach the classes as well. This helps make for a varying schedule of classes. Afraid of feeling cooped up in a classroom when you are supposed to be on vacation? The classroom's windows take up half the walls and face the ocean and Cascade Head. The classroom

Hand-blown glass floats and art at Volta Glass Gallery.

kitchen is certified professional and doesn't skimp on any modern amenities.

Plenty of attractions and activities can be found in Lincoln City. The **Connie Hansen Garden** is a wonderful way to be outside if the wind on the beach is rough. The meandering paths lead past azaleas, rhododendron, flower shrubs, and many other hearty plants cherished by Connie for the 20 years she spent creating this lush 1-acre retreat. When it's time to head indoors for your art, check out the **Bijou Theater.** Originally opened in 1937, it is owned by folks who love their movies and cinemas. The programming is mostly the same films you'll find in the big cities, with some classics or local film festivals thrown in. Before each movie begins, an owner or employee stands in front of the audience and introduces the film, sharing any of its tidbits. This is one of those few movie theaters that serves freshly popped popcorn with authentic clarified butter.

One of the biggest yearly events in Lincoln City is **Finders Keepers,** a hunt for handblown glass floats on the beach. From October to Memorial Day, over 2,000 of these colorful floats are hidden by carefully selected resident volunteers. Each object is numbered and, once found, can be registered at the local visitor's office. The lucky finder also receives a certificate of authenticity and information about the artist responsible for its creation.

Lodging in Lincoln City is plentiful and priced for all budgets. From resorts to cottages and condos to inns, it's all there. In the off-season, travelers can roll the dice and take a chance on finding the room they desire once they get to town. But during the summer months or a holiday, reservations are almost necessary. On the south side of town is **The Water's Edge.** Its on-the-water condos offer a full kitchen, a balcony, and convenience—the perfect place to stay if you don't need room service or a front desk. And since some of the units are privately owned, it's quiet. Bring in the binoculars from the car. The view directly out the balcony is of Siletz Bay, with the ocean to the right. In the bay are tall rocks that are volcanic reminders of a time long ago. Pelicans, cranes, egrets, and sea lions are plentiful when the tide is low. Three waterways (Drift Creek, Siletz River,

The beach north of Lincoln City.
LAURA STANFILL

Enjoy the view but watch your step. LAURA STANFILL

Salmon River) meet the ocean at this bay and, because it is semi-enclosed, it's technically an estuary.

If you'd like to extend this trip a bit, the world's smallest navigable harbor, **Depoe Bay,** is just 11 miles south on US 101. This is the spot to find a whale-watching cruise. Pods of gray whales come through here 10 months out of the year. If the tide and wind are right, **Spouting Horn,** a naturally occurring sea geyser, can shoot up to 60 feet in the air and absolutely drench any person or car directly under the spray.

Additionally, there's loads of shopping and dining for such a tiny town, so you might want to linger a little.

IN THE AREA

Accommodations

An Exceptional Place B&B, 1213 SW 52 Court, Lincoln City. Call 1-866-994-4920. Ocean views. Located at south end of town, a quiet area. Web site: www.anexceptionalbandb.com.

Brey House, 3725 NW Keel, Lincoln City. Call 541-994-7123 or 1-877-994-7123. Ocean views. All rooms accommodate up to two guests and include a full breakfast. Web site: www.breyhouse.com.

Captain Cook Inn, 2626 NE Highway 101, Lincoln City. Call 541-994-2522 or 1-800-994-2522. A charmingly restored 1940s motel. Some rooms have full kitchens, including utensils.

Chinook Winds Casino Hotel, 1501 NW 40th, Lincoln City. Call 541-994-3655 or 1-877-4-BEACH1. An oceanfront hotel that is next to but not attached to the casino. The casino features monthly top-name concerts, a golf course, and a children's arcade. Pets allowed in nonsuite rooms. Web site: www.chinookwindscasino.com.

Historic Anchor Inn, 4417 SW Highway 101, Lincoln City. Call 541-996-3810 or 1-800-582-8611. The oldest hotel in Lincoln City, perpetually being restored as a labor of love. Community kitchen, no microwave or refrigerator in the lodge suites. Cabins are pet friendly. Web site: www .historicanchorinn.com.

Nordic Hotel, 2133 NW Inlet, Lincoln City. Call 541-994-8145 or 1-800-452-3558. Free WiFi, Sundeck; floodlights illuminate the surf each evening. Web site: www.nordicoceanfrontinn.com.

Oregon Beach Vacations. Call 1-800-723-2383. Over 200 beach rental condos and homes from Astoria to Florence. Able to handle requests such as gourmet kitchens, hot tubs, and specific views. Pet friendly. Web site: www.oregonbeachvacations.com.

Sea Gypsy, 145 NW Inlet, Lincoln City. Call 541-994-2552 or 1-800-452-6929. Offers the lowest beach access in Lincoln City. Indoor pool and sauna. Web site: www.theseasgypsymotel.com.

Water's Edge Waterfront Condos, 5201 SW Highway 101, Lincoln City. Call 1-800-723-2383 (Oregon Beach Vacations). Bay view. Full kitchen in all units; some have washer/dryer. Great spot for families. Available condominium layouts. Web site: www.oregonbeachvacations.com.

Attractions and Recreation

Antique Week, early February. Has a different theme each year; in the past has included citywide antique sales, a vintage fashion show and silent handbag auction, silent movies, historical tours, and a special drop of antique Japanese floats. Held throughout Lincoln City. Check with Lincoln City Visitor's Association for more details.

Barking Dog Farms, 4310 South Drift Creek Road, Kernville. Call 541-994-8341. Certified organic and a member of Oregon Tilth. Open from the end of May through Oct. Web site: www.barkingdogfarm.com.

Bijou Theater, 1624 NE Highway 101, Lincoln City. Call 541-994-8255. Real butter on real popcorn in a restored movie theater owned by movie lovers. Mostly new films but specials can include musicals, silent, classics, etc. Web site: www.cinemalovers.com.

Blue Heron Landing Motel and Marina, 4006 NE West Devil's Lake Road, Lincoln City. Call 541-994-4708. Rent canoes, hydrobikes, motor- and paddle boats. Web site: www.blueheronlanding.net.

Catch the Wind, 266 SE Highway 101, Lincoln City. Call 541-994-9500. If it's on a string and flies in the wind, it's here: classic kites, artistic kites, windsocks, and pinwheels. Web site: www.catchthe wind.com.

Chinook Winds Casino Resort, 1777 NW 45th Street, Lincoln City.

Call 1-888-244-6665. Open 24 hours with Las Vegas–style gaming. Ocean-view restaurant, all-you-can-eat buffet, snack bar, childcare, and arcade. Web site: www.chinookwindscasino.com.

Chinook Winds Golf Resort, 3245 NE 50th Street, Lincoln City. 18-hole course, indoor driving range, and restaurant. Web site: www.chinookwinds casino.com.

Connie Hansen Garden, 1931 NW 33rd Street, Lincoln City. Call 541-994-6338. Open daily from dawn to dusk. Web site: www.conniehansengarden.com.

If you can avoid summer weekends, you may have the beach to yourself.
LAURA STANFILL

Finders Keepers, October through Memorial Day. Each year, 2,000+ handblown glass floats are hidden on the beaches of Lincoln City. The lucky finder can then register it with the Visitor Center and receive a certificate of authenticity and information about the artist. Don't bother asking anyone where the floats are. The locals are very secretive about them, in the interest of fairness.

Jennifer L. Sears Glass Art Studio, 4821 SW Highway 101, Lincoln City. Call 541-996-2569. Make a personal memento of the Oregon coast or simply watch others make theirs. Reservations are needed during the summer months. Insured shipping is available. Web site: www.lcglass center.com.

Kite Festival, June and October. Lincoln City Skate Park, Kirtsis Park, NE 22nd Avenue and Reef Street, Lincoln City. Competitive kite enthusiasts come from as far away as Japan, Australia, South America, and Europe to display their kites and demonstrate their skills on Lincoln City's windy beaches. The 8,000-square-foot facility has more than 100 lines and a unique 9-foot "cradle" to challenge skateboarders of all levels.

The Little Antique Mall, 3128 NE Highway 101, Lincoln City. The largest antique mall on the Oregon coast. Call 541-994-8572. Web site: www.littleantiquemall.com.

Mossy Creek Pottery, 483 Immonen Road, Lincoln City. Call 541-996-2415. Web site: www.mossycreekpottery.com.

North by Northwest Books & Antiques, 6334 South Highway 101, Lincoln City. Call 541-994-3087.

North Lincoln County Historical Museum, 4907 SW Highway 101, Lincoln City. Call 541-996-6614.

Robert's Books, 3412 SE Highway 101, Lincoln City. Call 541-994-4453.

Surf City Classic Car Show, September. Chinook Winds Casino Resort parking lot. All ages welcome. Live entertainment.

Tanger Outlet Mall, 1500 SE East Devil's Lake Road, Lincoln City. Call 541-996-5000 or 1-866-665-8680. Outdoor outlet mall. Web site: www .tangeroutlet.com.

Dining

Barnacle Bill's, 2174 NE Highway 101, Lincoln City. Call 541-994-3022. Not a sit-down restaurant but an open-air market selling cooked and raw local seafood. The seafood cocktails are tangy and fresh.

Blackfish, 2733 NW Highway 101, Lincoln City. Call 541-996-1007. Highly reviewed (Sunset Magazine, Travel & Leisure) casually elegant dining. Be sure to try a homemade Ding Dong for dessert. These are only available for those dining in, no take-out. Web site: www.blackfishcafe .com.

Humble Pie Pizzeria, 1114 NE Highway 101, Lincoln City. Call 541-994-4840. Pizzas whole or by the slice, homemade cookies and pies. Graffiti is encouraged. Take-out strongly recommended due to lack of tables.

Otis Café, 1259 Salmon River Highway, Otis. Call 541-994-2813. Very casual and small. In the warm months, there are tables are outside, too. Prepare for a wait during weekends.

Pronto Pups, 1252 Salmon River Highway, Otis. Call 541-996-4844. An Oregon original (Rockaway Beach), Pronto Pups have been around 60 years and these are the same corn dogs as sold at state fairs around the nation.

Rockfish Bakery, 2733 NW Highway 101, Lincoln City. Call 541-996-1006. A rare find on the coast, this bakery makes artisan breads and fantastic cinnamon rolls. The lunch menu is small, but fresh ingredients on great bread make for a swell bite. Web site: www.rockfishbakery.com.

Wildflower Grill, 4150 North Highway 101, Lincoln City. Call 541-994-9663. The breakfasts are wonderful; lunch and dinner, too. The marionberry cobbler is the best on the coast. If the weather is nice, ask for the patio. It's surprisingly quiet considering how close it is to the highway.

Other Contacts

Lincoln City Visitors Authority, 801 SW US 101, Lincoln City. Call 1-800-452-2151. Web site: www.oregoncoast.org.

Lincoln City Cultural and Visitor Center, 540 NE Highway 101, Lincoln City. Call 541-994-8378. Web site: www.lincolncityarts.org.

The dedication statue at Jessie M. Honeyman State Park.

CHAPTER

3

Sand Dunes on the Coast

Florence to Bandon

Estimated length: 65 miles
Estimated time: 5 hours to 2 days

Getting There: From I-5 (where it intersects with Eugene, Oregon), take I-105 west and follow it as it turns south. Turn west on West 11th Avenue. This street becomes OR 126. Just keep going west until Florence. Take US 101 south until Coos Bay. From downtown Coos Bay, head west on Central Avenue, which turns into Ocean Boulevard SE. Turn west on Newmark Avenue toward the shore and Cape Arago Highway. From here, Seven Devils Road take you back to US 101 and on to Bandon. In Bandon, take Beach Loop Drive for 5 miles and connect back with US 101.

Highlights: Right out of the gate, this trip starts with a side trip to **Darlingtonia State Wayside.** Only 5 miles north of Florence, it's the state's only park dedicated to a single plant species, which also happens to be the only carnivorous plant in Oregon. Also called cobra lilies, these otherworldly looking plants grow contentedly in a bog with easily navigable platforms built upon it. It's a short walk, perfect for children, and there's no entrance fee. These interesting little bug eaters are protected, so please don't pick any as a keepsake. The road continues on to Sutton Lake; though it's picturesque, it has mostly private residences with no public services.

US 101 is considered one the world's most favored highways. For all

It's a short side trip to see Oregon's only carnivorous plant.

of its 397 miles in Oregon, the road boasts uncomplicated driving and remarkable views. However, between its summer visitors and the fact that the highway is the main street of most of the towns along the coast, be prepared for periodic congestion. Begun in 1920 and finished by 1936, 101 was initially called the Theodore Roosevelt Coast Military Highway. The original purpose is purported to have been as a way for military to move unencumberedly to prepare to protect the West Coast, if necessary.

At the junction of OR 126 and US 101 is the north entrance to the **Oregon Dunes National Recreation Area,** a 47-mile-long stretch of nature's remarkable beauty. The wind on the Oregon coast can be relentless but it's also a creative carver, keeping the sand dunes an ever-changing work of art. A dune can move 6 or more feet in a year, sometimes up to 18 feet. Half of the 14,000 acres are open to off-road vehicles and other recreational activities—dune buggying, horseback riding, hiking, sailboarding. For a better view of these magnificent towers of sand (the highest can rise to nearly 500 feet high), consider taking a guided dune buggy tour. **Sand Dunes Frontier** offers fast-moving tours for the adrenaline pumped, as well as tours that move slower and even stop for photo ops. And as they're only half an hour long, it's easy to schedule one into your busy day at the coast. Tours or vehicle rentals are on a first-come, first-serve basis, with allowances for the weather. Still want to enjoy the dunes close up? Known as the first sandboard park in the world, **Sand Master Park** encompasses 40 acres of private sculpted sand dunes, with ramps and rails for tricks plus a pro shop. Instructors are on hand to teach you the basics, but call ahead to make sure of their availability. Think of sandboarding as snowboarding with no snow.

Golf lovers know the Scottish origins of the game but not all get to play those historic courses. The courses along this trip have dunes, ocean views, and wind suggest a near-Scottish golf experience. These same attributes produce an environment of a hardy golf game. The scenery, wildlife, and native landscaping of some of the more expensive courses here have been compared to Scotland's beloved but intimidating Carnoustie, as well as to Pebble Beach in California. There are nine courses from Florence to Bandon, located 30 miles south.

The town of Florence might better have been named Venice: it sits among a latticework of water: not just the Pacific but also 15 lakes, and the Siuslaw River, which flows 150 miles before hitting the ocean. Florence is popular with fishers of Chinook, steelhead, and sturgeon. The town's location makes it very popular with outdoor activity lovers. What's not clear is whom the town was named after. Officially it's said to honor A. B. Florence, a state senator of the mid-1800s. But there are those who say it was named after a French ship that wrecked at the Siuslaw River's mouth in 1875. Whatever the inspiration, Florence is a busy town offering lots to see and do, as well as spots where you can relax and watch the tides come in.

Lovers of books find a lot to adore in Oregon. It seems that every region of the state is birthplace to, the setting of, or the inspiration for, a slew of cherished books. Two miles east of Florence along the Siuslaw River is Cox Island, a salt marsh and estuary reserve now owned by the Nature Conservancy. Among all the great features this group and their volunteers are preserving on the 187-acre, environmentally important piece of land is the house that is said to have inspired Ken Kesey's *Sometimes a Great Notion.* The Benedict House is over 100 years old and has seen better days. But to Kesey it was to be the book's Stamper House.

Just before you drive across the Siuslaw River, venture into Florence's historic Old Town shopping district by veering off Highway 101 and following the signs. The area can get a little busy on summer weekends. It's a pedestrian-friendly area replete with boutiques, shops, restaurants, and inns. Many Oregonians are familiar with **Mo's Seafood Restaurant.** That's because they've been going there for chowder since childhood. But although it's a traditional dining destination along the coast (there are three of them) and very family friendly, it's not necessarily the best choice for cuisine. If you can take the time, try the **Bridgewater Restaurant,** whose chowder and crab melts deliver what's expected of these coastal dining staples. Their hand-dipped onion rings and herbed brown rice are welcome additions to the menu's local standards. If you're at the northeast end of Old Town and smell a sweet and tempting aroma, it's most likely the caramel corn made on-site at **Sure Beats Farmin.'** The nostalgic smell has the ability to waft directly up to you and lure you in as in an old Warner Brothers cartoon. And the **Beachcomber Tavern** serves a good burger in a biker-bar atmosphere.

To see much of the Florence area in one grand swoop, you'll need to book a flight with **Aero Legends.** As long as you're not afraid of flying and maybe a few bugs in your teeth, the flight in a 1944 Stearman Kaydet takes you past some of the more memorable sights, including Heceta Lighthouse 11 miles north of town. With all the water in and around Florence, a trip with **Oregon by Kayak** presents you the view from the water, as opposed to from the shore. The guided trips can be a full or half day in flat or moving waters. If taking to the water or skies isn't for you, get to know Florence's history at the **Siuslaw Pioneer Museum** in historic Old Town.

In and around Florence, there's more shopping and dining than just

The Edwin K. B&B in Florence is a true Sears and Craftsman home.

that found in Old Town. **Nature's Corner Café Market** serves healthy and sustainable foods made fresh and on premises. Popular dishes can run out, so don't be put off by the specials menu's crossed-out items. It's a tight squeeze in the parking lot and in the café, but the food is worth it. There's also a grocery area in the same tight space; you might also want to stop by for the market's original picnic options and car snacks. To see the work of a variety of local artists under one roof, check out the **Backstreet Gallery.** There's a lot to choose from here, from paintings to handmade cards to books from local authors.

During the third weekend of May, Florence is home to the **Annual Rhododendron Days** festival. The first Florence "rhodie" celebration took place in 1908, before many of the roads were even paved and when the population was only 500. It's the third-oldest flower festival in the West, including the Tournament of Roses in Pasadena, California. With the exception of during both world wars, the festival has taken place consistently, even through the Great Depression. Now as then, the pink and white wild blooms remind residents and visitors that the rejuvenating spring has finally arrived at the rainy Oregon coast.

Oregon has more than 200 historic bridges eligible for the National Register of Historic places. Built in 1936, the Siuslaw River Bridge was constructed at the end of famous architect Conde B. McCullough's tenure as the state's official bridge engineer. The Siulsaw River it spans is roughly 110 miles long and feeds the Siuslaw Estuary. Although the Siulsaw is not quite as popular as other area rivers, kayaking and bird-watching at the estuary are making it more so.

Three miles south of Florence is an attraction that Oregon's families can't get enough of, **Jessie M. Honeyman State Park.** The quote on the bronze statue dedicated to the park's namesake makes this perfectly clear: "No work is more important than teaching the children that the God-given beauty of Oregon is their heritage." There's everything for outdoor fun, from 500-foot-high white sand dunes for exploring, to freshwater lakes for swimming and fishing. The many camping options make this a busy spot. And though there are crowds, the park is very well set up. As the second-largest overnight camp in the state (almost 400 sites), you'll find tents, RVs, and yurts. Of the two lakes here, Lake Cleawox is best for swimming, whereas Lake Woahink is best for boats and renting canoes. Siltcoos Spring helps fill the area with color from the wild pink rhododendrons it nourishes, and you can go huckleberry and blackberry picking as summer ends and fall approaches. In the 1950s, *Life* magazine named this one of the top 10 state parks in the nation. And staying here is a bit nostalgic. If you are looking to camp on or near the beach, this is not the spot for you. It's a 2-mile hike to shore. But with all there is to do here, the ocean may not be too missed.

At milepost 201, the **Oregon Dunes Overlook** has a paved ½-mile trail to viewing decks. Should you decide to take up the trail again and venture away from the decks, the path is unpaved and more difficult. Watch for signs alerting you to the habitat of the snowy plover. This endangered sparrow-size shore bird is shy, especially when nesting. Nearby is Tahkenitch Lake. The lake was an ocean estuary until 3,000 to 4,000 years ago, when earthquakes separated it off from the Pacific, which now lies 1.6 miles away. Fishes here include largemouth bass, yellow perch, crappie, bluegill, cutthroat trout, and steelhead.

On your right, just before the bridge into Reedsport, is the very serene

Bolon Island Tideways State Scenic Corridor and Umpqua River. There's a hiking trail that goes halfway around the small island and ends in a bird-roosting area. Should you come across trees whose branches have been decimated by the droppings from cormorants, don't be alarmed. The weighed-down and corroded branches break off and become excellent fertilizer for future plants and fauna. Ain't nature's natural cycle grand? There is no drinking water on the island, so be sure to pack some for the hike.

Closer still to the town of Reedsport, you'll cross over Smith River, named for Jedediah Smith, the first white man to cross the Sierra Nevada. He made other remarkable "firsts" trips but died at only 33 years old. Although it's a bit of a detour, the **Dean Creek Elk Viewing** area is wonderful for those hoping to get a good look at some elk. Located 8 miles east on OR 38, it encompasses 1,040 acres, much of which is manipulated to make it more palatable to the elk. The area is open year-round and has roughly 60 to 100 head in the herd. From about mid-May and into June, the cows and calves seek higher ground, so there may be fewer elk to see then. Keep an eye out for bald eagles and blue herons here, too.

Back in town, the **Umpqua Discovery Center** teaches how tidewaters influenced the cultures that lived here and their impact on the environment. The center also has displays concerning the time when logging and canning were the lifeblood and money of the region. Once everyone's had enough education, go skate or watch at the town's 11,000-square-foot skate park. Designed by Airspeed Skate Parks, the main attraction is the Funnel Tunnel that, when built, was thought to have been the only funnel-shaped full pipe. If you like your feet firmly planted on the ground, take a walk around the dike that surrounds the middle of town. Park near the Visitor Center, where OR 38 and US 101 meet, and head toward the north side of the parking lot. Not only is it a gentle walk but you'll get surprising views of the Scholfield Slough. A visit to **The Bee Hive** before getting on your way is suggested. Not astonishingly, it's about honey here. The owner has been a professional beekeeper for over 50 years and provides the raw, local, pure honey from his bees. The flavored versions can range from blackberry to raspberry to clover and are available in different sizes. There are taste samples, too. The gift shop carries honey-based products such as lip balm and soaps, as well as nuts and dried fruit from local growers. The store is a not-for-profit whose proceeds help families in need of food.

Four miles farther south is Winchester Bay. To get there, leave OR 101 at Eighth Street. Consider taking some of Oregon's catch home: stop by for cans of albacore tuna from **Sportsmen's Cannery and Smokehouse.** The trawl-caught tuna canned here is sustainable and tests show it has lower mercury levels. Salmon Harbor is well known for sports fishing charters from February to mid-May. Whale-watching excursions can be found in the same harbor. Continuing on Salmon Harbor Drive to Lake Marie is an easy jaunt; it is stocked annually with trout. Just a bit farther is the **Umpqua River Lighthouse,** the first lighthouse commissioned on the Oregon coast. Tours are available from May through September; outside of those months, you'll have to be satisfied with enjoying the lighthouse's exterior only. It is the second lighthouse on this site, first illuminated in 1894, replacing the original built in 1857, which was lost to flooding. It's unique in Oregon, thanks to its red and white lights that flash day or night. The red light can be seen from up to 19 miles out at sea. Inside are about 1,000 hand-cut prisms imported from Paris. The prism glass isn't red because the

For many it's all about the reel and rod.

pigment couldn't take the heat. The color was achieved with a brass plate that moves in unison with the light, and which holds plates of glass that are covered in pigeon blood and gold flecks—perhaps a little unsettling to think too deeply about but very effective visually. The former Umpqua River U.S. Coast Guard Station next door now serves as the Coast Visitor Center and Lighthouse Museum; upstairs is an art gallery.

To get back to US 101, you'll have to double back the way you came. Once back on the highway, you'll pass a few lakes—Clear Lake, Lake Edna, and Teal Lake. Then comes William M. Tugman State Park, which has campsites and yurts year-round and is not as busy as many other area parks. The park surrounds Eel Lake, a good spot for catching bass weighing up to 5 pounds. Like the name says, the town of Lakeside sits on the shore of Ten Miles Lake. This lake is really two lakes connected by a channel and is also known for good bass fishing—so good that tournaments are held nearly every weekend, March through September. At Tenmile Creek you can find salmon, steelhead, and Chinook. There was a time when Clark Gable used to like to fish here. The town does have such services as markets, gas, and lodging.

Found on Oregon's southern coast, the myrtle tree is an evergreen laurel that produces a wood harder than oak or black walnut, with unusual and attractive hues of reds, black, browns, yellows, and greens. Just before North Bend, off OR 101 via Sandy Way, is the **Myrtlewood Factory Showroom.** Although the name has changed a few times, they've been around since 1911. Along with bowls, kitchen accessories, home décor items, and small furniture, the store also carries raw myrtle wood for hobbyists.

Entering into North Bend, you'll cross McCullough Bridge, Oregon's longest coastal bridge at 5,305 feet long, which spans Coos Bay, the largest deep draft port between San Francisco and Puget Sound. Fresh oyster lovers pay heed: on average, 2.5 million tons of oysters move through the Port of Coos Bay annually. Once you've crossed the first half of the bridge, you'll want to head northeast on Bay Road to **Clausen Oysters,** Oregon's largest oyster producer. They have a retail shop where you can have an oyster shooter or purchase fresh shucked oysters to go. If your room has a kitchenette or your campsite a barbecue pit, going to Clausen is a delicious and inexpensive way to enjoy this seafood. And because these oysters are in water too cold for them to spawn, they are firm and tasty whatever the season. If oysters aren't a favorite, how about pancakes or pie? From the outside, the **Pancake Mill** looks like a run-of-the-mill coffee shop but inside it's anything but. For almost 30 years, they've been making fresh pies, real-deal waffles, and genuine Swedish pancakes. For a coffee shop, the menu also has a fairly varied vegetarian section. Be sure not to miss the monthly pie specials. You wouldn't want to miss out on any of the sour cream pies. Once you're full of baked goods, learn more about ship building and shipwrecks at the **Coos Historical and Maritime Museum,** located in Simpson Park. The museum contains over 40,000 artifacts. The tales of shipwrecks are simultaneously interesting and strangely romantic.

At over 16,000, Coos Bay is the largest city on the Oregon coast. The Coos Bay Boardwalk runs parallel to US 101 and has plenty to look at and learn from. The ½-mile or so walk is a combination of wood walkway and paved trail. Historical displays and two retired tugboats will help you glean how important the bay was and is. Classic film lovers in town during a weekend should not miss the **Egyptian Theater.** From musicals to horror films, it's all about great movies being shown in an outstanding old picture palace built in 1925. It has been lovingly restored by community volunteers. The Egyptian theme, architecture, vaudeville history, and all-around cool vibe make seeing any movie here a true treat. The **Coos Art Museum** is Oregon's third-oldest museum of this type and specializes in Northwest artists and contemporary American printmakers. Here you'll find the Prefontaine Memorial Gallery, dedicated to the gifted Olympic runner and Coos Bay native Steve Prefontaine.

In Coos Bay, the **Old Tower House** is not only quaint but well located, too. After you spend a comfortable night in this bed & breakfast, the next leg of your journey starts just minutes from its front door. Built in 1872, the house is the oldest structure in the county and the proprietors are happy to share their knowledge of the first three owners and the colorful history of the home, all of which helps to add to the experience of staying here. The grounds and garden are well kept and feature 100-year-old apple trees rescued from a shipwreck over a century ago. On these grounds, in addition to the main house, a perfectly private and cozy cottage sits. Its private entrance and driveway make your coming and going your business alone. Inside are a separate sitting room, bedroom, and full bath. The convenient arrangement works well for busy families, romantic couples, and those interested in privacy. Breakfast is served on a dreamy veranda but the cottage also has a large front parlor with ample seats by the fireplace, and a formal dining room. There are three more guest rooms in the main house; all are upstairs and decorated with Victorian antiques.

The cottage on the grounds of the Old Tower House in Coos Bay offers extra privacy at the B&B.

Next is the harbor community of Charleston. It's a small, picturesque spot with year-round clamming at the South Slough Bridge. If you'd rather someone else catch your meal, stop by the **High Tide Café**. It's a no-nonsense kind of place that serves better food than that often found in swanky seafood restaurants. The dress code is nonexistent, deck dining overlooks the slough, and the rock fireplace inside helps chase the chilly damp away. Their pan-fried oysters will make you think that maybe uprooting and moving to the Oregon coast is the thing to do. If you've had it up to here with seafood, beef stroganoff and several kinds of steak are also on the menu. And save room for dessert—any of them; they're all great. Unfortunately, High Tide has a noisy dining room, and if you happen here when there's live music, a conversation is practically out of the question. Oh well; you shouldn't talk with your mouth full anyway.

From Charleston, head west on the Cape Arago Highway. First up is **Bastendorff Beach Park,** a 2-mile-long flat beach that is very family friendly and a swell spot for kite flying. In the rocks at the south end are tide pools. And at the north end is the South Jetty, which offers some shelter from the wind, perfect for just lying around. Near the jetty may not be best for swimming families, though, due to riptides. About a mile farther down the highway is the **Cape Arago Lighthouse.** This is the youngest of the Oregon lighthouses (1934) but that's due to its being the third incarnation at this locale. Two others built on the same site (1866 and 1908) were victims of weather and erosion. This one isn't open to the public for tours. The best place to see the lighthouse is at the viewpoint just over a mile south.

Sunset Bay State Park is available for day use or overnight. What makes this park worth a stop are the hiking trails that connect you to Cape Arago. Along the trail you'll have marvelous views of Gregory Point and Cape Arago Lighthouse. There are also tide pools teeming with life, and plenty of sandy beaches. That official viewpoint for Cape Arago Lighthouse is ¼ mile past this park.

Shore Acres State Park is the pride and joy of the area, and well it should be. The 743 acres were once the spot of the grand summer home of an early timber baron. The original mansion was lost to fire and its replacement is gone, too. But between the formal gardens, pond, and two rose gardens, the park seems have something blooming almost year-round. If you're in the area for Christmas, be sure to stop by for the holiday light display. Inside the park is a fully enclosed glass observation deck, making winter storm watching comfortable and much safer. (Is storm watching exciting? It is in the Pacific Northwest.) Look also for the meadow where Malcolm Forbes took off in a hot-air balloon in 1973, making the first transcontinental air balloon flight. There's a plaque commemorating the occasion.

Just over a mile south are **Seal Lion Lookout and Simpson Reef.** This overlook provides views (if the sea mist isn't too heavy) of Shell Island,

Simpson Reef, and the protected wildlife there. You may be able to see the northern elephant seal and harbor seal, as they reside here year-round. To see (or hear) a California or Steller sea lion, the best times are late summer and early fall. Gray whales are close enough to glimpse when they swim to Alaska from March to June, or again from December through February, when they swim back toward Baja, California. If you're visiting the lookout between Memorial and Labor days, you could be fortunate and come upon the group Shoreline Education Awareness. These docents are chock-full of information on the wildlife here; with the help of their telescopes, you can almost count the seals' whiskers. Should you come across a lonely seal pup, please leave it be. Its mom is off getting food and will return. Each year, people mean well by "rescuing" a pup, but it is rarely in distress and removing it from its natural habitat could have disastrous results.

Cape Arago was once known as Cape Gregory and was named by Captain Cook. In 1850 the name was changed to honor a French geographer and physicist, François Dominique Arago. Also named after him are one of Neptune's rings and a crater on Mars. Fossil fiends will want to check for

Volunteer docents help explain the area's wildlife at Seal Lion Lookout.

Simpson Reef and Shell Island through the ocean mist.

low tide here. This is also the farthest north Sir Francis Drake ever got on the North American continent, having reached here in June 1579. At the park, trails lead down the cliffs to three coves—South, Middle, and North. At Middle Cove, sandstone from the Eocene era remains in the large boulders. In these boulders or in the area exposed by the low tides, marine fossils such as crabs, gastropods, and occasionally sand dollars have also been found. If you're going for some serious fossil digging, a permit is required for anything beyond a 3 by 6-inch-deep hole. The South Cove trail leads to tide pools. The North Cove trail is best for viewing offshore colonies of seals and sea lions, but is closed March through June for their birthing season. Be sure to check the tide table charts before hiking down to the narrow beach. They are available at many shops and lodging facilities, as well as in the local paper. To return to US 101, doubling back along Cape Argo Highway to Charleston is necessary. From there, continuing on Seven Devils Road will take you back to US 101.

You've returned to the cute town of Charleston, which is also the entrance to the **South Slough National Estuarine Research Reserve,** the first estuarine reserve in the nation (designated in 1974). In total, it's 4,800 acres of freshwater streams, upland forest, salt marshes, mudflats, open water channel, nature trails, boardwalk, and tide flats. Travel 4 miles on Seven Devils Road, at the west end of Charleston, to reach free maps and information about the trails, tide pools, wild life, cultural exhibits, and a short film on the estuary. A mile farther south, you'll come to the south entrance to the reserve. From Charleston back to US 101, via Seven Devils Road, is 11 miles. After 9 miles, a turnoff will direct you to Seven Devils and Whiskey Run Beach. The latter is well known to agate hunters, though in the 1850s it was a gold mining camp with the largest population in Oregon. All that's gone now. Pursuing agates is best after the outgoing tide.

Seven more miles south on US 101, **Bullards Beach State Park** has what many consider the best feature any Oregon beach can have: protection from the rarely ceasing wind. Once you park, you will need to travel more than a mile to the beach, but the trail is paved and open to bikes. The area is popular with surfers as well as those seeking out the Coquille River Lighthouse at the south end of park. Built in 1896, it was decommissioned in 1939. There are some historical displays and a small gift shop. Volunteers conduct tours April through October. During these months, the tower is open but the lighthouse may be closed for renovations.

And this brings you to Bandon (sometimes called Bandon-by-the-Sea), the last town on this trip. Like so many Oregon towns, Bandon was devastated by fire (in 1936), which destroyed most every business and many residences. In town, a brick chimney at the site of the old bakery stands as a memorial. Today the town is welcoming and ideal. It's not as closely packed together as other coastal towns, perhaps due to the terrain. The beaches are replete with lovely monolithic rock formations that have been carved into unique shapes by thunderous waves. The most famous is Face Rock. Often when a rock formation is named after what was seen in its façade, the turtle or maiden, or whatever it is, is difficult to make out. Not so with Face Rock. It looks as if film special-effects legend Ray Harryhausen dreamed it up for *Jason and the Argonauts* or *The Seventh Voyage of Sinbad.* Make no mistake, you will see the face, which looks as if a giant of the sea has awakened from his long slumber.

Among other things, Bandon calls itself Oregon's Cranberry Capital. All told, about 5 percent of the nation's cranberries are grown here, which comes out to be roughly 30 million pounds annually. Luckily enough, in 1885 a gold seeker by the name of Charles McFarlin didn't have any success with panning gold, so he turned to the cranberry vines he'd brought from Massachusetts. Bandon also calls itself the Storm Watching Capital of the World. One thing is for sure: this town of just over 3,000 is home to three highly reviewed golf courses—Bandon Dunes, Pacific Dunes, and Bandon Trails.

For interesting shopping, the **Gypsy Wagon** is as colorful as a store can get. And after some gray coastal days, the perks acquired from perusing the jewelry, tapestries, sculptures, clothing, and much more from around the world are appreciated. The owner's background is in cultural anthropology and she stocks the store with rare and unusual ethnic pieces. One of the best natural scents is ocean air and lavender. At **Merritt Lavender Farm,** organic practices are used to grow the aromatic flowering plant. Tours are available by calling ahead, and a small gift shop carries such products as infused vinegar and essential oil.

The legendary **Bandon Fish Market** deserves all the praises heaped upon it—for a location on the pier, clam chowder with plenty of clams, scrumptious fish and chips, and a zesty Dungeness crab cocktail. There's no real seating inside except a few stools, but there are tables outside. Views are an added benefit at many restaurants, but if the food isn't good, then the view is wasted. What about no view but splendid food? The **Wild Rose**

Bistro follows the philosophy of the "slow food" movement, providing a menu that focuses on local seasonal ingredients and only wild seafood, never farm-raised or frozen. Still want a view? Go for a walk.

To make the most of your time in Bandon, head to Kronenberg Beach. Just look for signs saying "Beach Loop Drive" in Old Town or take 11th Street off US 101 and follow it to Beach Loop Drive. Here you'll find paths with interpretive signs, wooden staircases, seastacks (tiny offshore islands), and an area great for bird-watching. Keep an eye out for endangered tufted puffins out on the rocks. Each spring after a winter alone at sea, the birds return to the same mate and nest. At **Bandon Beach Riding Stables,** you can take that iconic horse ride on the beach. However, here, all trips are guided. Also, from here you can see the aforementioned Face Rock.

If you're heading back to I-5 from Bandon, you'll be traveling on OR 42. For a great burger, stop by small town of Coquille and the **Coquille Broiler.** If you'd rather pack your own sandwich, the Sandy Creek Covered Bridge is a swell picnic spot. The picnic tables on the bridge make it unique, even in the state with most covered bridges in the west and one of the most in the nation. Sitting under the short bridge's roof, rain or shine, adds charm to any meal. Leave OR 42 at the town of Remote and go ¼ mile.

IN THE AREA

Accommodations

Coos Bay Manor Bed & Breakfast, 955 South Fifth Street, Coos Bay. Call 1-800-269-1224. Pet and children friendly. Web site: www.coosbay manor.com.

Edwin K Bed & Breakfast, 1155 Bay Street, Florence. Call 541-997-8360 or 1-800-833-9465. A 1914 Sears Craftsman home with six rooms. Stay includes an enormous breakfast and afternoon tea. Web site: www.ed wink.com.

Fish Mill Lodges & RV Park, 4844 Fish Mill Way, Westlake. Call 541-997-2511. On Siltcoos Lake, 5.5 miles south of Florence. Two-night minimum for RVs. Six cabins and four rooms also available. Web site: www.fishmill.tripod.com.

Jessie M. Honeyman State Park, 3 miles south of Florence. Call 1-800-452-5687. Open year-round with tents, RVs, cabins, and yurts. Web site: www.oregonstateparks.org.

Old Tower House Bed & Breakfast, 476 Newmark Avenue, Coos Bay. Call 541-888-6058. A perfectly located historic home with rooms in the main house and a guest cottage.

Oregon Beach Vacations, Florence, Bandon, Charleston, Coos Bay, North Bend, Winchester Bay. A wide variety of beach rentals from condos to homes. Web site: www.oregonbeachvacations.com.

Park Motel, 85034 Highway 101 South, Florence. Call 541-997-2634 or 1-800-392-0441. A classic motor motel surrounded by pine trees and 5 acres of lawn and gardens. Two-room cabins available, too. Web site: www.parkmotelflorence.com.

Port of Siuslaw RV Park Marina, 100 Harbor Street, Florence. Call 541-997-3040. 105 RV sites, some on the water. Web site: www.portof siuslaw.com.

Siltcoos Station Retreat, on Siltcoos Lake, 5½ miles south of Florence. Four attached 1930s lakefront cottages. E-mail for reservation rates and availability: SiltcoosStation@lanecc.edu. Web site: www.lanecc.edu/florence/siltcoos/.

Umpqua State Lighthouse Park. Call 541-271-4118 or 1-800-452-5687. 64 sites including cabins and yurts.

Attractions and Recreation

Aero Legends, Florence Municipal Airport, Florence. Call 541-991-6139. Fly in an open cockpit biplane over Florence and Heceta Head Lighthouse. Web site: www.aerolegends.com.

Backstreet Gallery, 1421 Bay Street, Florence. Call 541-997-8980. Co-op gallery featuring local artists. Web site: www.florenceartists.com.

Bandon Beach Riding Stables, 54629 Beach Loop Road, Bandon. Call 541-347-3423. A guided 3-mile ride lasts about an hour and leaves four times a day. May through September, a sunset ride is available. Reservations strongly recommended.

Bandon Crossings Golf Course, 87530 Dew Valley Lane, Bandon. Call 541-347-3232. A "favorite hidden gem" of the PGA guide. Web site: www.bandoncrossings.com.

Bandon Dunes, 57744 Round Lake Drive, Bandon. Call 1-888-345-6008. Ranked one of the top 100 courses in the world by *Golf Magazine*. Web site: www.bandondunesgolf.com.

Bandon Face Rock Course, 3235 Beach Loop Road, Bandon. Call 541-347-3818. Water comes into play at eight on the nine holes.

Bandon Glass Art Studio and Gallery, 240 Highway 101, Bandon. Call 541-347-4723. Glass sculpture, as well as blown glass, from a variety of artisans. Web site: www.bandonglassart.com.

Bandon Historical Museum, 270 Filmore, Bandon. Call 541-347-2164. Housed in the second building built after the first museum perished in a 1936 fire. Web site: www.bandonhistoricalmuseum.org.

The Bee Hive, 1041 Highway 101, Reedsport. Call 541-271-2571. Specializes in local honey and honey-based products; the store's proceeds help feed hungry families.

Blackberry Arts Festival, Coos Bay. Last weekend in August. Web site: www.coosbaydowntown.org.

C'est Vert, 175 SE Second Street, Bandon. Call 541-329-0189. Repurposed jewelry and art as well as organic gourmet foods. Web site: www.cestvert.com.

Central Coast Water Sports, 1901 Highway 101 North, Florence. Call 541-997-1812. Learn to boogie board, kayak, and dive, with equipment rental and instructors. Locally owned and operated by native Florence folks. Web site: www.centralcoastwatersports.com.

Clausen Oysters, 66234 North Bay Road, North Bend. Call 541-756-3600 or 541-267-3704. Bring your own cooler to keep your oysters in or enjoy oyster shooters on the spot. Web site: www.silverpointoysters.com.

Coos Art Museum, 235 Anderson Avenue, Coos Bay. Call 541-267-4877. Third-oldest art museum. The permanent collection focuses on Northwest artists. Web site: www.coosart.org.

Coos Historical and Maritime Museum, 1220 Sherman Avenue, North Bend. Call 541-756-6320.

Coquille River Lighthouse, Bullards Beach State Park, 2 miles north of Bandon. Call 541-347-2209. Open to tours May through Oct.

Cranberry Festival, Bandon. Early September. Web site: www.bandon cranberryfest.com.

Cranberry Sweets & More, 280 First Street, Bandon. Call 541-347-9475. Web site: www.cranberrysweets.com.

Dean Creek Elk Viewing Area, north of Reedsport on OR 38. Open year-round.

Egyptian Theater, 229 South Broadway, Coos Bay. Call 541-269-8650. Classic movies shown Fri. through Sun. in a remarkable 1925 theater. Web site: www.egyptiantheater.org.

Faber Farms, 54982 Morrison Road, Bandon. Call 541-347-1166. A working cranberry farm open to the public. October is harvest time.

Forest Hills Country Club, 1 Country Club Drive, Reedsport. Call 541-271-2626. Nine regulation holes.

Gypsy Wagon, 155 SE Baltimore Avenue, Bandon. Call 541-347-1775. The front of the store is designed to look like a Middle Eastern open-air market and features items from around the globe. Closed Tues.

Joy of Quilting, 2970 Highway 101, Florence. Call 541-902-8863. Along with fabric, notions, patterns, and books, the store carries a large selection of batiks. Web site: www.joyofquilting.net.

Ken's Rod and Reel Repair, 984 Laurel Avenue, Reedsport. Call 541-271-1921. No graphite rods found here.

Kentuck Golf Course, 675 Golf Course Lane, North Bend. Call 503-756-4464. Near an inlet; creeks and ponds are at most holes.

Merritt Lavender Farm, 87450 McTimmons Lane, Bandon. Call 541-347-7190. Open to the public June through Dec., closed Wed. and Sun. Web site: www.lavenderladyfarm.com.

Mill Casino, 3201 Tremont, North Bend. Call 541-756-8800 or 1-800-953-4800. Live gaming, entertainment, lodging, and RV park. Web site: www.themillcasino.com.

Myrtlewood Factory Showroom, 68794 Hauser Depot Road, North Bend. Call 541-756-2220. Web site: www.realoregongift.com.

The Myrtlewood Gallery, 1125 Highway 101, Reedsport. Call 541-271-4222. Web site: www.myrtlewoodgallery.com.

Ocean Dunes Golf Links, 3345 Munsel Lake Road, Florence. Call 541-997-3232. The course is built on a natural sand base and is irons only. Web site: www.oceandunesgolf.com.

Old Bandon Golf Links, 3235 Beach Loop Drive SW, Bandon. Call 541-329-1927. Reconditioned nine-hole public course. Web site: www.old bandongolflinks.com.

Oregon by Kayak. Call 541-729-2436. Guided tours of the Siuslaw River or Siltcoos. Web site: www.oregonbykayak.com.

Oregon Coast Historical Railway, 766 South First Street, Coos Bay. Call 541-297-6130. Restored steam and diesel locomotives on display, along with memorabilia. Web site: www.orcorail.com.

Oregon Divisional Chain Saw Sculpting Championships, Reedsport. Father's Day weekend. Web site: www.odcsc.com.

Port O' Call, 155 First Street, Bandon. Call 541-347-2875. Boat rentals and charters. Web site: www.bandonportocall.com.

Rhododendron Festival, Florence. Second weekend in May. Call 541-997-3128. Web site: www.florencechamber.com.

Sand Dunes Frontier, 83690 Highway 101 South, 4 miles south of Florence. Call 541-997-3544. Take a guided tour or rent a dune buggy or ATV. Web site: www.sanddunesfrontier.com.

Overlooking the bay, Fishpatrick's restaurant features its own putting green.

Sand Master Park, 87542 Highway 101 North, Florence. Call 541-997-6006. Free admission with any rental. Web site: www.sandmasterpark .com.

Sandpines, 1201 35th Street, Florence. Call 541-997-1940. Rated 4½ stars by *Golf Digest.* Web site: www.sandpines.com.

Sea Mist Winery, 86670 Croft Lake Lane, Bandon. Call 541-348-2351. Oregon's first cranberry winery. Call ahead for tasting and tour information. Web site: www.seamistwine.com.

Shore Acres Park, Cape Argo Highway, 4 miles from Charleston. Web site: www.shoreacres.net.

The Shorebird Festival, Charleston. Last weekend in August, headquartered at the Oregon Institute of Marine Biology. Web site: www.fws.gov /oregoncoast/shorebirdfestival.htm.

Siuslaw Pioneer Museum, 278 Maple Street, Florence. Call 541-997-7884. Closed for Dec.

Sportsmen's Cannery and Smokehouse, 182 Bayfront Loop, Winchester Bay. Call 541-271-3293. The perfect Oregon coast souvenir: locally caught and canned tuna. Web site: www.sportsmenscannery.com.

Sunset Bay Golf Course, 11001 Cape Arago Highway, Coos Bay. Call 541-888-9301. Easy-to-walk nine-hole course.

Umpqua Discovery Center, 409 Riverfront Way, Reedsport. Call 541-271-4816. Learn how life in and around the region is at the will of the tides. Web site: www.umpquadiscoverycenter.com.

Umpqua River Lighthouse, 1020 Lighthouse Road, Winchester Bay. Call 541-271-4631.

The Wool Company, 990 SE Second Street, Bandon. Call 541-347-3912. Yarn and knitting/crochet supplies. Closed Sun. Web site: www.wool company.com.

Dining

Bandon Boatworks Restaurant, 275 Lincoln Avenue SW, Bandon. Call 541-347-2111. Fresh seafood and a view of the Coquille River.

Bandon Fish Market, 249 First Street, Bandon. Call 541-347-4282. Practically no seating inside, but the food is worth standing up for. Web site: www.bandonfishmarket.com.

Beachcomber Tavern, 1355 Bay Street, Florence. Call 541-997-6357. Juicy burgers in a boisterous yet friendly tavern.

BJ's Ice Cream, 2930 Highway 101 North, Florence. Call 503-997-7286. Pleasant and busy, with their own handmade ice cream and original flavors.

Bliss' Hot Rod Grill, 1179 Highway 101, Florence. Call 541-997-6726. A '50s-style diner at which old cars have been outfitted for dining.

Bridgewater Restaurant, 1297 Bay Street, Florence. Call 541-997-1133. Try the hand-dipped onion rings or crab melt.

Coquille Broiler, 2 North Central Boulevard, Coquille. Call 541-396-7039.

Marionberry pie at the Pancake Mill in North Bend.

Fishpatrick's Crabby Café, 196 Bayfront Loop, Winchester Bay. Call 541-257-2512. A traditional café with salmon fish and chips.

High Tide Café, 91124 Cape Arago Highway, Charleston. Call 541-888-3664. Seafood, including fish and chips made of halibut or white fish. Cozy fireplace indoors and an outdoor deck with a view. Web site: www.hightidecafellc.com.

Krab Kettle, 280 Highway 101, Florence. Call 541-997-8996. Specializes in fresh local fish.

Lord Bennet's Restaurant and Lounge, 1695 Beach Loop Drive, Bandon. Call 541-347-3663. Web site: www.lordbennets.com.

Outdoor In, 305 Fourth Street, Coos Bay. Menu includes pizza and sandwiches. There's an arcade and indoor playground. Web site: www.outdoor-in.com.

Nature's Corner Café Market, 185 Highway 101, Florence. Call 541-997-0900. Deli-style café with fresh, organic, and sustainable ingredients. Breakfast and lunch only.

Pancake Mill, 2390 Tremont Street, Highway 101, North Bend. Call 541-756-2751. A superb coffee shop with freshly baked items. Web site: www.pancakemill.com.

The Tea Cozy, 95 West 11th Street, Bandon. Call 541-347-4171. Web site: www.theteacosy.com.

Waterfront Depot, 1252 Bay Street, Florence. Call 541-902-9100. Tapas and small plates. Best to make reservations.

Wild Rose Bistro, 130 Chicago Avenue, Bandon. Call 541-347-4428. What it lacks in ocean view, it more than makes up for with fresh seafood and local ingredients.

Other Contacts

Lane County Convention and Visitors Association, 754 Olive Street, Eugene. Call 1-800-547-5445. Web site: www.travelanecounty.org.

Oregon Dunes National Recreation Area Visitor Center, 855 Highway Avenue, Reedsport. Call 541-271-6000. The center is closed on weekends during the winter.

One of the 14 glorious waterfalls in Silver Falls Park.

CHAPTER

4

Falls 'n' Creeks 'n' Rivers

Marion and Linn Counies

Estimated length: 225 miles
Estimated time: 5 hours if driving straight through, or 2 full days

Getting There: Leave I-5 at Woodburn exit 271, head east following the Silver Falls Tour Route signs. This becomes OR 214, though it changes names—to Wilco Highway and Hillsboro Silverton Highway. Be sure to veer to right at Woodburn Monitor Road and on to Mount Angel. Continue south on OR 214 from Mount Angel, to Silverton and then Silver Falls. Here the highway turns west to OR 22. Drive east on OR 22. Once in Sweet Home, head west on Highway 228. This will return you to I-5, less than 50 miles south of the point you exited.

Highlights: The rain that falls in the Willamette Valley, starting each late fall and continuing until late spring, is worth weathering through. After the rain departs northwestern Oregon, the state is left with waterfalls, temperate rainforests, lush greenery, and scores of beautiful stops along the road.

Although the first stop doesn't have a beautiful waterway to enjoy, the town of **Mount Angel** (population 3,755) is no less lovely to look at. The Kalapuyan tribe named this area Tapalamaho (Mount of Communion) as it was their spot for communion with the Great Spirit. In 1882, at around the same time Bavarian immigrants were settling the area, a house of the Order of Saint Benedictine was formed by a contingent of monks from Engelberg, Switzerland. The **Mount Angel Abbey** was established here in 1884 and included a seminary. Sadly, fires destroyed the original wood buildings, as well as the basalt replacement. The current monastery was built in 1928. Architecture fans will want to pay close attention to the seminary library designed by "the father of modernism," Alvar Aalto. Located atop a 485-foot butte, the abbey provides an astounding view of the fertile Willamette Valley below, and sometimes of Mount Hood and Mount Saint Helens. A walking path that follows the driveway features Stations of the Cross tableaux. The abbey's museum is open daily, and along with liturgical vestments, its collection includes Civil War memorabilia, natural history artifacts, and some unusual items. Two popular favorites are the stuffed carcass of a six-legged bovine calf and what is suspected to be the largest bezoar—or hog hairball—in the world.

A woodcarver craftsman works on the new sign for Mount Angel's public library.

On the way to and from the abbey, you'll pass **St. Mary Church,** which was completed in 1912. Built in a Gothic revival style, the church has 22 stained-glass windows, the 2 largest of which were made in Munich, Germany.

Not far behind the brothers at the abbey were the Benedictine sisters of Mount Angel. The original building at the **Queen of Angels Monastery** was completed in 1888. Originally a school, the monastery is now the **Shalom Prayer Center** and Benedictine Nursing

Center. The latter is now managed by an outside hospital group. The Shalom gift and bookstore carries spiritual books, inspirational and meditative music, prayer shawls, children's items, and the award-winning Monastery Mustard (formerly named Benni's Mustard, after St. Benedict). Made from a closely guarded old family recipe, the mustard is adored and cherished. The garlic version has taken second place in world mustard competitions three times since being sold to the public in 2005. For a more in-depth look around the property and buildings, pick up a map and a list of building descriptions at the bookstore. And July through October, iris rhizomes named for the monastery are sold as a fundraiser.

Each September, Mount Angel holds one of the largest **Oktoberfest** festivals in the country. If the slow rhythm of a small town is what you seek, it's best to stay away during these four days. It's estimated that nearly 350,000 people make the trek to this tiny spot for the Bavarian-style food, dancing, entertainment, and of course, beer.

Much of Mount Angel's downtown is decorated in a traditional German, Swiss, or Bavarian style. The most eye-catching is the **Glockenspiel Restaurant,** designed to look like an Alpine chalet. Fifty feet above the front door, the **Mount Angel Glockenspiel** depicts hand-carved renditions of the area's historically important folks—the Kalupuya brave praying to the Great Spirit, Mathias Butsch who brought the monks, Sister Bernadine Wachter, homesteaders Robert and Katrina Zollner, Prior Adelhelm Odermatt who named the town, and the Oktoberfest mascot, Papa Oom Pah. The finale is on the next level up, where two traditionally dressed Bavarian children swing and "sing" "Edelweiss."

After the show, head across the street to the **Mount Angel Woodcarver's Association's Der Schnitzerwerkstatt.** In this tiny storefront you'll find an array of pieces from dozens of different local wood artists, including some from those who worked on the glockenspiel. The woodworkers are very happy to talk about their group and art form. The merchandise spans from Native American–influenced works to a classic Saint Nicholas. It's a great spot to pick up a unique souvenir. On the corner south of the store is another type of wood art, **Der Maibaum.** Displayed in front of city hall, this maypole—called the Tree of Trades—pays tribute to all that was and is the foundation of Mount Angel.

The **Glockenspiel Restaurant** looks like it may just be a tourist trap but the food, décor, and service are well worth your walking in. The menu offers traditional Bavarian items with a local twist. The spaetzle is served with a tangy mustard cream sauce and the fondue comes with Oregon's crisp apples. If a quick bite in a casual atmosphere—a kind of brat 'n' beer spot—is what you're looking for, try **Mount Angel Sausage Company.** Choices include bratwurst, fricadelwurst, knackwurst, smoked wurst, and more. There's indoor and outdoor seating and plenty of good German beers to choose from. Although the restaurant is family friendly, you may wish to take your food to **Humpert Park** for an impromptu picnic.

Once you leave Mount Angel, you'll be heading south on OR 214 again. About 2 miles out of town, **Gallon House Bridge** is one of Oregon's 51 covered bridges. Originally built in 1916, it cost $3,000 to construct. At one time, Silverton was a dry town and Mount Angel was not. The bridge provided a spot to drop off jugs of alcohol, also known as a "pigeon drop." To get to the bridge, go west on Hobart Road. After ½ mile, turn north on Gallon House. The bridge is open to cars but you'll have to make a three-point turn around to return.

Silverton is a town with spunk and individuality to spare. The vibrant downtown has varied shopping and dining, public art murals, and the first pet parade in America. Lodging here runs the gamut from quaint bed & breakfasts to traditional motels. Not traditional and well worth consideration is **The Oregon Garden Resort.** Its rooms are in small, condo-style clusters. All are situated on the ground floor and parking is just outside your door. The rooms are tasteful and not overly stuffy. The grounds and landscaping are very well maintained. Along with a restaurant is a welcoming lodge-style lounge, complete with roaring fire and live entertainment. Although only the staff are locals, the vibe is friendly and includes sing-alongs. The resort's location, adjacent to **The Oregon Garden,** is a horticulturist's dream and guests can use the hotel's own entrance to the garden. This means no searching for parking or waiting in line to enter. A shuttle picks up just outside the hotel on a regular basis, but if it's a splendid morning, walk over before the garden is open to the public. The Oregon Garden features 20 different inspiring display gardens spread out over 80 acres.

Just as you turn your car into the Oregon Garden driveway, renowned architect Frank Lloyd Wright's **The Gordon House** can be seen hiding amid the high grasses. Reasonably priced guided tours are available but reservations are highly recommended. This is Wright's only house in Oregon and his only one open to the public in the Pacific Northwest.

There are two famous names in Silverton's past: renowned cartoonist

The Oregon Garden Resort rooms offer balconies, privacy, and easy access to the Oregon Garden.

Homer Davenport and Bobbie, the Prodigal Dog. Davenport was a famous political cartoonist during the last the turn of the century. Although he lived most of his adult life outside of Oregon, he is still celebrated every year at the **Homer Davenport Days** held each August. The family-friendly event includes customized davenport races and a political cartoon competition. Bobbie was a collie owned by a Silverton couple. When they were visiting Wolcott, Indiana, in 1923, the pup got separated from his owners. He traveled more than 2,800 miles in over 6 months but eventually found his hometown. His story made national headlines and resulted in his own silent movie. To pay tribute to this long-trekking collie, the **Silverton Pet Parade,** the nation's oldest of this type, is held in town each mid-May. A mural, elaborate doghouse, and statue dedicated to Bobbie can be found downtown, where there are also 12 other hand-painted **murals**. The subjects range from the Silverton Red Sox (at one time, a farm team for the Boston Red Sox) to another resident hero, International Space Station astronaut Don Pettit.

In Silverton, you can see both types of theater: live and film. The **New Palace Theater** was built in 1936 to replace an opera house that was lost

The statue and house are dedicated to a collie who walked thousands of miles to come home.

to fire. It's now owned by the current mayor of Silverton. First-run films play here and at shockingly low prices. Classic plays, as well as new ones, can be enjoyed at the **Brush Creek Playhouse.** Built in 1888, it was originally a schoolhouse and has been the local theater for over 30 years. Be forewarned: There is no proper restroom in the building.

The fertile lands in the Willamette Valley are producing some exciting and award-winning wines. Although many of the local wineries are not directly on this route, many are worth the time taken for a small side trip.

Stop by the Silverton Chamber offices for a map from the **East Valley Wineries and Vineyard Association.** Then contact the wineries individually to see if they're currently open to the public for tastings or tours.

Continue on OR 214 heading south, following the signs to **Silver Falls Park,** about 13 miles. This park is not only the largest state park in Oregon (9,064 acres), but with 14 waterfalls, it has the highest concentration of them in the United States. Five are more than 100 feet high and the highest reaches 178 feet. The facilities at the park are well maintained and include multiple restrooms, a volunteer-run retail store, and general maps posted near trailheads. There are 30-plus miles of trails at the park, the most beloved being the Trail of Ten Falls. This 7.8-mile trail takes hikers past six waterfalls and behind four. Plan on at least three hours to hike the entire trail. If time is short or the main parking lot crowded, veer to the right at the entrance. Follow the signs to North Falls Parking. The trail to North Falls from here is fairly easy but does require a steep incline on the return. The striking North Falls descend 136 feet, crashing onto huge basalt blocks. On this trail you can walk behind the falls. Upper North Falls can be accessed from that same parking lot (a map is posted) and it's just a 15-minute hike. This waterfall is only 65 feet high and can't be walked behind. Swimming under a waterfall isn't an option here; however, there is a lovely swimming hole. During July and August, temperatures can rise to the 90s and even triple digits.

Leave Silver Falls at the main entrance and continue on OR 214 until OR Highway 22. In about 15 miles, you'll come to the small town of Mehama. Here you'll find a sweet little spot to stop for ice cream, hot dogs, and a myriad of other fast-food items. The **Gingerbread House** may not be swanky but the service is warm and friendly. All menu items are available to go and though the patio is noisy due to the highway.

From OR Highway 22, there are two ways to approach the epic forests and clear waters of **Opal Creek Wilderness.** The simplest is to turn north at North Fork Highway, located just east of Mehama. Watch for a flashing orange light and the Swiss Village Restaurant. From there it's about 23 miles. But, miles and minutes can be shaved from your trip if you continue instead to the town of Gates and then take Gates Hill Road. Fair warning: This second option is a curvy road with some steep elevation.

Opal Creek Wilderness is one of a few old growth forests that have never been commercially logged. It was attempted here in the 1930s, but the two trucks fell down a cliff. Gold was found in 1859 and the area was

Three Pools in Opal Creek Wilderness.

mined until 1992. Some of the land and old growth area was donated to the Friends of Opal Creek. The group fought long and hard to have the rest of the surrounding area protected from future business interests, and in late 1996, the Opal Creek Act required that all privately owned lands be returned to public ownership.

If your interest in Opal Creek is a brief afternoon visit, then Three Pools and Shady Cove will be your destinations. A very easy and exceedingly short hike from the parking lot will take you to Three Pools. The running water here is some of the cleanest in the nation, some say the world. Shady Cove is another ½ mile farther along Forest Road 2207. Both provide awe-inspiring beauty. If hiking, no cell phone reception or Internet access, and strictly vegetarian meals are of interest, arrange to visit the **Opal Creek Ancient Forestry Center.** It's a 3-mile hike in to the updated cabins and lodge. Most are designed for large groups (10 or more) but there are a few options for smaller parties. Reservations should be made well in advance.

For those not interested in roughing it, the **Elkhorn Valley Inn** is located a few miles from the Opal Creek entrance and offers quiet serenity in an inviting atmosphere. Many bed & breakfasts seem to muscle in on your vacation time, but not so here. Owner Sharon knows how to make sure you have everything you desire without being invasive. This charming farmhouse has rooms and bathrooms that can be adapted to your needs— kids in a separate room or the same, two rooms but only one bathroom is necessary, and so on. If the idea of sharing your space doesn't attract you to this B&B, check to see if Rene's Cottage is available. Separate from the main house, this appealing one-time chicken coop has been renovated with all that an individual, couple, or small family could want. A living room, kitchenette, fireplace, high ceilings with knotty pine beams, king-size bed, sofa bed, hot tub, and claw-foot bathtub provide spaciousness and comfort. Breakfast can be served on the back deck of the main house, which overlooks sprawling forests and mountains. There isn't a single building to block this astonishing view. Close attention is paid to the meal, from the quality coffee and bacon to the locally grown berries on your freshly made waffle.

Just a few miles west of the inn is the **Elkhorn Valley Golf Course.** Originally one of the best-rated nine-hole courses; the back nine has recently been completed and getting rave reviews. The course is about the game of golf, not a fancy clubhouse. As out of the way as this scenic and challenging course is, it's best to call ahead for a tee time, just in case.

The Elkhorn Valley Inn exudes warmth and true hospitality in a nostalgic country home.

As you continue to head east on OR 22, you'll come to the small town of **Gates.** This town of 505 citizens has two things going for it: an inexpensive Mexican restaurant that makes its own salsa and an honest-to-goodness steakhouse with a live bird show. At **Sierra Mexican Restaurant,** you won't find authentic Latin folk art or blue corn tortillas, but you will find straightforward food at very reasonable prices. The owners are on hand, so service is sincerely caring. At **Frontier Country Restaurant,** you can get prime rib and enjoy watching the birds in their aviary. Sounds like something in Las Vegas or Tampa, right? There's even a trout pond on the property, though not in the restaurant.

About 10 miles farther east on OR 22 is **Detroit Lake State Park.** Before 1953 there was no lake here, but once the Detroit Dam was put in, the 400-foot-deep lake quickly became a popular destination for Oregonians. The average summer water temperature is 78 degrees and the lake has swimming spots at the Mongold and Flats day-use areas. Fishing enthusiasts can find rainbow trout, Kokanee, landlocked Chinook, and sometimes bullhead catfish.

The first views of Mount Jefferson can be seen at the Mount Jefferson Vista. At milepost 48, turn south and head toward the parking area. There are views here of the reservoir as well as the mountain. This spot is also recommended for seeing western and horned grebes, common loons, hooded and common mergansers, along with the occasional bald eagle.

As OR 22 heads south, after the towns of Detroit and Idanha, places to stop for food, lodging, and gas will be sparse for the next 100 miles or so, so be sure to prepare for this leg of your journey. This highway here leads through higher and higher elevation. Due to the altitude, the Douglas fir trees begin to dissipate and the white fir and Ponderosa pines start to speckle the land. You will also start to see black lava rock, which is about 3,000 years old and originated at the nearby Nash Crater.

Marion Forks Fish Hatchery near milepost 66 is open to the public, though there are no tours. Here Chinook salmon and steelhead eggs are incubated and raised for release at the Detroit and Big Cliff dams, to make amends for both hydroelectric dams having contributed to the loss of habitat and blocked migration paths. This spot is also on the Oregon Cascades Birding Trail. Blue grouse, mountain quail, hermit warbler, rufous hummingbird, Hammond's flycatcher, belted kingfisher, and red-breasted sapsucker have been spotted here.

At the junction of OR 22 and OR 20, head west on 20 toward the town of Sweet Home. Not long after the junction is the parking and trailhead for the **Hackleman Old-Growth Trail,** a 1.8-mile graveled trail takes you to trees more than 500 years old. The trail loops at Hackleman Creek, which has a subspecies of cutthroat trout that were isolated from their brethren in the McKenzie River by lava flows nearly 10,000 years ago.

Keep a lookout for milepost 52 and two historical markers. This section of Santiam Highway has been a busy thoroughfare for some time. Much of the highway runs parallel to the Santiam Wagon Road, built in 1869 to take settlers from Willamette Valley to Central Oregon. This was a toll road until 1915. In 1905, the route was also part of the first Transcontinental

Auto Race from New York City to Portland, which took 44 days. There are spots on the original road where pre-1940 cars are allowed to travel. About ½ mile farther on the south side of highway is a wide lookout bridge that juts into the Santiam River. Along with being a swell spot to have your photo taken, the bridge is quite buoyant and moves up and down as you walk across.

Just outside the Willamette National Forest, **Cascadia State Park** is available for overnight and day use. The campgrounds are primitive and not too busy. Its options for swimming, hiking, fishing, and exploring are plentiful. The trail leading to Soda Fork Falls is only 1 mile long but does have a 150-foot ascent. At the turn of the last century, there was a grand hotel resort here, complete with bowling alley and tennis courts. You can still enjoy the stone patio but the other amenities are long gone. A second trail is paved and leads to where Soda Creek and the Santiam River meet. The wagon ruts from those looking to avoid the tolls of Santiam Wagon Road can be seen on this trail. The park is also a good place to leave your car and hike to **Cascadia Caves,** one of the oldest archaeological sites on the West Coast. The caves were used for over 8,000 years by more than one group, due to their location on trade and travel routes, along with nearby fishing spots. It's an easy 2-mile hike but if it's been raining recently, be sure to wear appropriate clothing and shoes.

Anglers of Oregon and the Pacific Northwest are very familiar with **Sweet Home.** With more than 8,500 residents, it's much bigger than most the towns on this road trip but may be the only one built atop a petrified forest. Two nearby reservoirs—Green Peter and Foster—teem with trout, Kokanee, and bass. There are also two museums in town: **East Linn Museum** and **White's Electronics.** The first centers on artifacts, photos, and tools dating back to 1852 and the pioneers, miners, and loggers so tied to the town's history. The latter is an odd collection of metal detectors and the stories that go with them, from a local company that has been making detectors, most of them by hand, for over 50 years. Rock hounds find the area around the town a treasure trove of crystals, agates (including the rarer colored ones), and jasper.

Petrified wood from maple, sycamore, oak, and 60 other tree species have been found at **Holleywood Ranch.** Whether you want to dig up your own or purchase one already unearthed, both are available and prices are determined by the weight of the piece. Tools are available for rental or you can bring own. The digs are available according to the weather but tend to start in early May. If you're tired of Northwestern cuisine, stop by **Spoleto's Pizzeria and Wine Shop** for pizza and fresh, giant salads. The cheese here is shredded by hand every day. If you still want that taste of Oregon, try the Portland Pesto pizza, which includes hazelnuts. After all, 90 percent of hazelnuts (many locals call them filberts) are grown throughout the state.

Campers and RVers will enjoy **River Bend County Park,** just east of Sweet Home. Although its location may be too close to civilization for some, the amenities are all brand new and it's an excellent place for families. Recently, almost 1 million dollars were spent on the park. The improvements include 90 sites, a playground, a ball field, showers, and a large picnic gazebo.

It's here in Sweet Home that you'll catch OR 228 for the rest of this trip.

At the west end of the quiet logging town of Crawfordsville sits the **Crawfordsville Bridge.** Like the town, it's named after Philemon Crawford, Crawfordsville's founder. Built in 1932, this open truss–style bridge went many years without regular upkeep. In the mid-1980s, volunteers cleaned it of weeds and overgrown bushes. A federal grant was also given for some renovations. In 1996, a flood damaged floor beams and tie rods. This time the grant to mend them came from the Oregon Covered Bridge Program.

One mile west of Crawfordsville is **McKercher County Park,** with ample parking, restrooms and picnic tables, plus easy access to the Calapooia River for swimming and fishing. If the rains have been hard and fast, the small falls are hidden and the waters become swift.

There are small towns that don't give any mind to whether travelers visit or not. Others know the value their history, architecture, and quaintness, and are happy to share it with anyone coming down the road. Thankfully, **Brownsville** falls into the second category. This town is Oregon's third oldest and its Main Street has many historical buildings and really emanates a feeling of simpler time. The film classic *Stand by Me* was filmed in and around here. The tree that housed the tree house in the film can be found heading straight up Main Street and making a right on School Avenue. The pie-eating contest scene was shot in Pioneer Park. The Brownsville Saloon was the scene for the Blue Point Diner. It's effortless to spend an afternoon walking up and down the main drag, shopping, eating, and sightseeing. Quite proud of its history, Brownsville holds events throughout the year, celebrating the past. **Carriage Me Back Day** features period-costumed actors and carriage rides. **Calapooia Croquet Court** is for

The Moyer House in Brownsville is open for tours most weekends.

anyone who loves or is interested in learning about the Victorian game. Equipment is provided. Oregon's oldest continuing celebration, the **Pioneer Picnic,** has been held in Brownsville every year since 1887. Originally the event was a reunion for Oregon Trail pioneers.

Not to be missed is the **Moyer House.** Construction on this elaborate Italianate villa–style home began in 1881. And though the house changed hands over the decades, even becoming apartments at one point, Linn County and volunteers have worked on bringing it back to its original grandeur, restoring the detailed woodwork both inside and outside the home, plus the ceilings and walls' hand-painted scenery found beneath wallpaper. Next to a small and quaint park is the **Linn County Historical Museum,** housed in the original railroad depot and boxcars. Its collection includes great treasures—one of only three extant Oregon Trail covered wagons, a boxcar movie theater, and a stuffed Oregon wolverine.

The unusual, odd, and quirky can be found anywhere and **Living Rock Studios** is one of Oregon's finer curiosities. For those who appreciate the beauty of rocks, this is where you can see jasper, thunder eggs, agate, and obsidian. The tree sculpture in the middle stands almost two stories high and the outside is made of petrified wood. There are also "windows" made of thinly sliced rocks put together make pictures of Bible stories, and a room with so many crystals it can be overwhelming. The building took more than 20 years to build and is still owned and operated by the daughters of the man responsible for the idea. It's one of those spots that could only have been dreamed up and accomplished by folks who adore Oregon, right down to the rocks.

Oregon's beauty, history, and originality abound in this trip. The waters refresh, the vistas inspire, the quaintness relaxes, and there are ample places to learn along the way.

IN THE AREA

Accommodations

Birdwood Inn, 511 South Water Street, Silverton. Call 503-873-3247. Three rooms and one suite. Lovely garden for morning coffee. Close to downtown. Web site: www.birdwoodbandb.com.

Cascadia State Park, Highway 20, 14 miles east of Sweet Home. Call 503-854-3406 or 1-800-551-6949. Open for camping Mar. through Oct. West-end park open year-round.

Cicily's Guest House, 5152 East View Lane, Silverton. Call 503-508-6796. A 1918 Craftsman bungalow for one to six guests. Web site: www .eastviewcountry.com.

Elkhorn Valley Campground, once in Lyons, turn east on North Fork Road from OR 22. Go 9 miles to the campground on the left. Call 503-375-5646. Open mid-May through Sept. First come, first serve, no reservation. All 24 sites have a fire grill and picnic table.

Elkhorn Valley Inn, 33016 North Fork Road SE, Lyons. The inn, innkeeper, and location in Elkhorn Valley—minutes from Opal Creek Wilderness—make this a wonderful place to rest after hiking, golfing, or doing nothing at all. Call 503-897-3033 or 1-800-707-3033. Web site: www.elkhornvalleyinn.com.

Fisherman's Bend Recreation Site, 27300 North Santiam Highway, Detroit Lake. Call 503-897-2406. This 170-acre campground is operated by the Bureau of Land Management and offers tent sites, as well as cabins. Web site: www.blm.gov.

Opal Creek Ancient Forest Center, Opal Creek Wilderness, Marion County. Call 503-892-2782. Cabins available for 2 to 50 people. A 3.5-mile hike to accommodations. Vegetarian meals available. Web site: www.opalcreek.org.

One of many varieties of gardens at the Oregon Garden.

Oregon Garden Resort, 895 West Main Street, Silverton. Call 503-873-5847. Located at the far end of the Oregon Garden, with an entrance just for hotel guests. Shuttle service to the garden is available. Web site: www.moonstonehotels.com.

River Bend County Park, 45931 Highway 20, Foster. Call 541-967-3917. Newly updated sites and amenities, close to Sweet Home. Web site: www.linn.co.us.

Silver Falls State Park Campground, 20024 Silver Falls Highway, Sublimity. Call 1-800-452-5687 for campsite reservations. Open mid-May through Oct. All 46 sites have a fire ring. Web site: www.oregonstateparks.org.

Frank Lloyd Wright's Gordon House in Silverton.

Silver Spur RV Park, 12622 Silverton Road, Silverton. Call 1-866-854-7785. Free WiFi and no-license fishing ponds. Web site: www.silverspurrvpark.com.

Silverton Inn & Suites, 310 North Water Street, Silverton. Call 503-873-1000. Web site: www.silvertoninnandsuites.com.

Water Street Inn, 421 North Water Street, Silverton. Call 503-873-3344 or 1-866-873-3344. Web site: www.thewaterstreetinn.com.

Whispering Falls Campground, 8 miles southeast of Detroit Lake. U.S. Forest Services campground. Open May through Sept. The waterfall is across the river located near the campground. Web site: www.fs.fed.us.

Attractions and Recreation

Blackberries, 215 North Main Street, Mount Angel. Call 503-845-2187. Victorian/country gifts, accessories, and furniture in a friendly and warm setting. Closed Sun. and Mon.

Bosnya's Butterflies, 208 Jersey Street, Silverton. Call 503-873-3032. Children's clothing boutique, carrying sizes infant to 14.

Brush Creek Theater, 11535 Silverton Road, Silverton. Call 503-873-5905. Live theater is performed in a former one-room schoolhouse that is over 100 years old. Web site: www.bushcreekplayhouse.org.

Calapooia Croquet Court, Pioneer Park, Brownsville. Call 541-466-5589. Come play croquet with provided equipment. Held Sun. and Wed., June through Oct. Web site: www.historicbrownsville.com.

Carriage Me Back Days, Brownsville. A one-day festival that includes carriage rides and actors dressed in the apparel of the chosen year. Web site: www.historicbrownsville.com.

Cooley's Gardens Peak Bloom Festival, 11553 Silverton Road Northeast, Silverton. Call 503-873-5463. The same family has been selling irises in the same location since 1928. The largest producer in the world of bearded irises. The best time to view the irises is mid-May to early June. Web site: www.cooleysgardens.com.

East Linn Museum, 746 Long Street, Sweet Home. Call 541-367-4580. Focusing on life in Sweet Home's pioneers, miners, and loggers. Closed Mon. and Tues. Web site: www.sweethomechmaber.org.

Elkhorn Valley Golf Course, 32295 North Fork Road, Lyons. Call 503-897-3368. Known as a golfing gem, hidden among stunning scenery. Originally a nine-hole course, the back nine was opened in 2000. Web site: www.elkhorngolf.com.

Eve's Rider Wear, 432 McClaine Street, Silverton. Call 503-873-0480. A boutique aimed at equestrian lovers. Web site: www.evesriderwear.com.

The Glockenspiel, 190 East Charles, Mount Angel. Call 503-845-6222. The West's tallest glockenspiel features hand-carved figures representing the groups in Mount Angel's history. The free six-minute show is given four times daily.

The Gordon House, 879 West Main Street, Silverton. Call 503-874-6006. A small and efficient house designed by Frank Lloyd Wright. Reservations are suggested but not always necessary. Web site: www.thegordonhouse .org.

The Gallon House covered bridge.

The Green Store, 201 East Main Street, Silverton. Specializing in sustainable and recycled items. Web site: www.silvertongreenstore.com.

Holleywood Ranch, 26250 Old Holley Road, Sweet Home. Call 541-405-5990. Dig up your own piece of petrified wood as a one-of-a-kind souvenir. Open seven days a week.

Homer Davenport Days, Silverton. Call 503-508-9591. An old-fashioned celebration centered around the famous turn-of-the-century cartoonist. Held early Aug.; includes an international cartoon contest. Web site: www.davenportdays.com.

Kriskindlmarkt, Mount Angel. This celebration includes a traditional European holiday market, tree lighting, and a visit from Kris Kringle. Web site: www.Mountangelchamber.org.

Linn County Museum, 101 Park Avenue, Brownsville. Call 541-466-3390. Open seven days a week. Web site: www.co.linn.or.us/museum.

Living Rock Studios, 911 West Bishop Way, Brownsville. Call 541-466-5814. Closed Mon.

Lunaria Gallery, 113 North Water Street, Silverton. Call 503-873-7734. A co-op gallery featuring local artists and a variety of mediums. Web site: www.lunariagallery.com.

Marion Forks Fish Hatchery. Call 503-854-3522. Hatchery for Chinook and steelhead supplied to Detroit Lake and Big Cliff Dam. Fee campgrounds are behind the hatchery.

Mount Angel Abbey, 1 Abbey Drive, Mount Angel. Call 503-845-3030. An excellent view, two museums, and a library designed by Alvar Aalto. Web site: www.mountangelabbey.org.

Mount Angel Oktoberfest, Mount Angel. A 45-year tradition, this is one of the largest Oktoberfests in the West. Each September, more than 350,000 people descend on this small town. Web site: www.oktoberfest.org.

Mount Angel Woodcarver's Association's Der Schnitzerwerkstatt, 125 North Garfield Street, Mount Angel. Call 503-845-9663. Closed Mon. Woodworking pieces from 25 artists, high-quality tools, and bass wood.

Mount Angel Wurstfest, Mount Angel. Call 503-845-6882. February marks the month that area sausage makers compete for bragging rights. Web site: www.Mountangelchamber.net.

Moyer House, Main Street, Brownsville. Call 541-466-3390. Tours are available of this elaborate 1881 home on weekends only.

Northstar, 209-B North Water Street, Silverton. Call 503-873-3891. More than 30 vendors offer antiques and collectibles.

Opal Creek Wilderness. Parking permit fee for daily use. Old growth forest that has never been commercially logged. Web site: www.opalcreek.org.

Oregon Garden, 879 West Main Street, Silverton. Call 503-874-8100 or 1-877-674-2733. Web site: www .oregongarden.org.

Palace Theater, 200 North Water Street, Silverton. Call 503-873-2233. First-run movies at an affordable price in a theater built in 1935.

Pioneer Picnic, Brownsville. Family fun, activities, and entertainment with a pioneer focus. Web site: www.historicbrownsville.com.

The Purl District, 201 East Main Street, Silverton. Call 503-873-6178. Yarn and notions for knitting and crochet enthusiasts. Open knitting group every Mon. evening.

Silverton may be a small town to some, but there's no shortage of hip shopping or dining.

Queen of Angels Monastery, 840 South Main Street, Mount Angel. Call 503-845-6141. The bookshop has a map for a self-guided tour around the historic grounds. Web site: www.benedictine-srs.org.

The Red Bench, 205 North Water Street, Silverton. Call 503-873-6555. Immense store, selling new items and antiques.

Silverton Pet Parade, Silverton. Call 503-873-5615. Each year on the Saturday in mid-May, the nation's oldest pet parade (est. 1932) moves through downtown.

Silverton Poetry Festival, Silverton. Call 503-873-2480. Readings by published and novice poets are held throughout Silverton each April.

Silver Falls State Park, 20024 Silver Falls Highway, Sublimity. Daily entrance fee. Detailed trail maps can be found at the Web site and retail store just in the main entrance. Web site: www.oregonstateparks.org.

St. Mary's Church, 575 East College Street, Mount Angel. Call 503-845-2296. Built in 1912; the stained-glass windows and towering spire are worth a look.

Stomp, 208 East Main Street, Silverton. Call 503-873-9400. Hip organic clothing, handmade accessories, and European shoes.

Stone Buddha, 216 East Main Street, Silverton. Call 503-873-0682. Asian imports, including home décor, incense, toys, and clothing.

Trinity Lutheran Church, 500 North Second Street, Silverton. Call 503-873-2635. Make an appointment for any day of the week to see the church's 90-year-old stained-glass windows.

White's Electronics Museum, 1011 Pleasant Valley Road, Sweet Home. Call 541-367-6121 or 1-800-547-6911. Dedicated to the company's mostly handmade metal detectors. Open during regular business hours.

Dining

Bavarian Haus, 115 East Church Street, Mount Angel. Call 503-845-9466. Lunch and dinner with seasonal patio dining. Closed Mon.

Cedar Shack, 4102 Highway 20, Sweet Home. Call 541-367-5841. Home of the infamous Spotted Owl Burger.

Frontier Country Restaurant, 714 Highway 22, Gates. Call 503-897-2960. Serving burgers, roasted chicken, and steaks, with an aviary for entertainment. Open for lunch and dinner. Closed Mon. Web site: www.frontiercountryrestaurant.com.

Gingerbread House, 21935 Gingerbread Street, Mehama. Call 503-859-2247. Enormous ice-cream cones, creamy shakes, and seasonal elk burgers.

Glockenspiel Restaurant, 190 East Charles, Mount Angel. Call 503-845-6222. Well-known German and Bavarian restaurant with moving glockenspiel hand-crafted clock above the front door. Web site: www .glockenspielrestaurant.net.

Mac's Place, 201 North Water Street, Silverton. Call 503-873-2441. Lunch and dinner. The outside deck looks over a small river. Web site: www.woodennickel.com.

Mount Angel Sausage Company, 105 South Garfield, Mount Angel. Call 503-845-2322. Laid-back atmosphere with walk-up service and plenty of good beers. Lunch only. Web site: www.ropesausage.com.

O'Brien's Café, 105 North Water Street, Silverton. Call 503-873-7554. Serves breakfast and lunch.

Poppa Al's, 198 Highway 22, Mill City. Call 503-897-2223. This simple joint provides burgers on homemade buns and the shakes.

Rolling Hills Bakery Café, 106 North First Street, Silverton. Call 503-873-8489. Freshly baked items and lunch.

Sierra Mexican Restaurant, 302 Highway 22, Gates. Call 503-897-9911. Fresh salsa and low prices.

Silver Grille Café & Wines, 206 West Main Street, Silverton. Call 503-873-4035. Dinner only.

Spoleto's Pizzeria and Wine Shop, 4804 Highway 20, Sweet Home. Call 541-367-4001. Pizzas and calzones come with classic or Northwest-style original toppings.

The Point, 6305 Main, Sweet Home. Call 541-367-1560. A family-style restaurant with view of Foster Reservoir from its dining room and patio.

Other Contacts

Mount Angel Chamber of Commerce, 5 North Garfield Street, Mount Angel. Call 503-845-9440. Web site: www.Mountangelchamber.org.

Silverton Chamber of Commerce, 426 South Water Street, Silverton. Call 503-873-5615. Web site: www.silvertonchamber.org.

Travel Salem Visitors Center, 181 High Street NE, Salem. Call 503-581-4325. Web site: www.travelsalem.com.

Many u-pick farms can be found along this trip. LAURA STANFILL

CHAPTER

5

Not So Far from the City

Washington and Yamhill Counties

Estimated length: 47 miles
Estimated time: 4 hours to 2 days

Getting There: From 217, leave Scholls Ferry Road and head west for about 8 miles. Take a left on OR 210, which becomes OR 219/Southwest Hillsboro Highway. This connects with SW Bald Peak Road. Continue on this road until Laurelwood, go west to OR 47, and head south toward Yamhill and McMinnville. From Carlton, go east on Hendricks Road and then south on Abbey Road. Once in Lafayette, take OR 99 east to Dayton or west to McMinnville.

Highlights: Not every adventure has to be far from the big city. Many a metropolis has great places to visit, just minutes away. And so it is with Portland, the largest city in Oregon, which has numerous scenic drives close by. They're quick to get to and back from, and can be easily done in a day. This trip takes you through smaller towns and communities west and southwest of Portland, on the west side of the Willamette Valley. This region is replete with wineries, fine restaurants, and soft rolling hills. From berry picking to French bistros, you can eat your way through every stop and still not sample all the bounty offered here.

This trip starts at the prettiest barn in Oregon, **Smith Berry Barn**. Here you'll find exquisite fresh produce and so much more. It's one of those places that carry all the things you didn't know you were looking for. Heirloom vegetable seeds, garden books, and handmade soaps are just a few of the products you'll find here. That isn't to say that it's a hodgepodge of stuff, all strewn about willy-nilly. This may be one of the nicest barns you've ever had the pleasure of shopping in. Everything is tastefully displayed in lovely arrangements, from the local gourmet foods to Smith's own raspberry-rhubarb jam. There's a patio to sit on as you enjoy most likely the best fruit milkshake you have ever tasted. Each day, the fruit that is unsold is frozen and used to make the cool treats. If you're looking to eat a proper meal before your milkshake dessert, head across the street to the **South Store Café.** Housed in a building over 100 years old, this café serves homemade soups, fresh salads, and sandwiches made with bread from a local

Smith Berry Barn has it all, including magnificent shakes. LAURA STANFILL

bakery. The décor is a mixture of artsy, vintage, and a tiny bit of unintentional country. The bright and airy dining room and friendly service make for a very comfortable experience—so comfortable, it takes awhile before you're back in the car and on your way.

Who knew there was so much to know about lavender, other than that bees like it and it smells so nice. At **Mountainside Lavender,** you can learn all about the sweet-smelling plant, stroll the peaceful grounds, and pick a lavender bouquet. The family-owned and -run farm has over 1,000 of the plants and in 20 different varieties. As you choose your lavender, be sure to look around: the farm offers views of Mount Hood, Mount Rainier, and the coastal range. Any interest in the making of lavender oil will elicit a detailed description and demonstration from the owners, the Carlsons. The range of products they make from their own plants ranges from lip balm to culinary lavender. The warm and forthcoming owners will be happy to share the tricks of the trade for growing your own successful lavender plants.

It's amazing that **Bald Peak** is rarely, if ever, crowded. Sure, there isn't anything fancy about the park, but there doesn't need to be; the view more than makes up for it. There's no need to hike—just drive up, park, and enjoy. And to top it all off, there's no fee. On an exceedingly clear day, you can face east for glimpses of the mountains St. Helen's, Hood, and Adams, far in the distance. Continue on SW Bald Peak Road to Laurelwood Road and go left (west), and in less than 8 miles you'll reach the small town of Gaston and OR 47. Two miles to the right (north) on OR 47 will bring you to the turn for **Scoggins Valley Park** and **Henry Hagg Lake.** The lake can be enjoyed in a myriad of ways. There are two boat ramps on the fully stocked lake and the western half of the lake is a no-wake zone. Picnic tables are found all around the lake; Scoggins Creek on the west end seems the most tranquil. There are 15 miles of hiking trails and observation decks for wildlife and bird-watching. The paved road leads all around the lake and makes for a pleasant 11-mile scenic drive.

As you pass south through Gaston, you can feel rest assured stopping for a bite at **Cooper D's,** a true "joint." The yakisoba is surprisingly good with fresh vegetables that, though cooked, still retain their crispness. There are also bison burgers and real fries and shakes. If they haven't run out, get the handmade pot stickers. For ambiance, try friendly: watch locals coming in, being greeted by name, and picking up their "regular" order.

There must be something magical in the water in Yamhill. This sweet,

The view from the rarely crowded Bald Peak. LAURA STANFILL

picturesque town of 800 has produced two award-winning and respected writers. The best known is children's book author Beverly Cleary. Her beloved stories about Ramona Quimby, Henry Huggins, and Ralph S. Mouse have been translated into 14 languages. Cleary spent her early childhood in the Queen Anne–style home on the edge of town before moving to Portland. The other writer is Pulitzer Prize–winning journalist and author Nicholas D. Kristof. His *New York Times* pieces and books have opened many a reader's eyes to the plights of different peoples around the world.

Pizza is one of those foods that you can find everywhere—but that doesn't mean you should eat it. But in such a tiny town as this, what's surprising is how good the pizza is at **Zippy's Pizza**. And it doesn't stop with the pizza. The homemade dessert pies are outstanding, though which flavors are available really depends on luck. Will they be peach, coconut cream, lemon cheesecake, or some other scrumptious variety? The wine and beer list is very locally oriented and very reasonably priced. Sit at the beautiful 1920s bar and enjoy a slice and a glass of wine. Zippy's also has tables and a small arcade for a family-friendly meal. The building dates from 1904, and thanks to the loft-style exposed brick and high ceilings, its old-fashioned ambiance has been retained.

Cooper D's is one of the few places in the tiny town of Gaston.

There's a revered shop in Yamhill. Revered by quilters, anyhow. **The Quilted Hill** stands overlooking rolling hills of wineries and farms, in a sweet cottage painted barn red. Best known for carrying lots of cotton fabrics at respectably low prices, the store was named one of the top 10 quilt shops in the United States by *Quilt Sampler* magazine. For quilters, coming here is a quest.

Unless your trip to this part of Oregon is completely winery focused, it can be difficult to make it to all the wineries, especially the smaller artisan ones. At **Carlton Winemakers Studio** in Carlton, the equipment inside is shared by multiple boutique winemakers, and at any one time, you may find up to 10 of them, with their respective wines available in the tasting room. Upon closer inspection, the unassuming building is actually very sleek and environmentally friendly. There isn't an official restaurant here, but each midweek, April through September, a celebrated local chef creates a three-course meal with wine pairings. Reservations must be made in advance.

In case you are still looking to satiate your wine-tasting palate, head to the smack-dab middle of Carlton. Here you'll find multiple tasting rooms and wine bars, most within strolling distance of one another. The **Tyrus Evans Tasting Room** was once a train depot and the **Scott Paul Wine's** tasting room is in a 1915 structure that was once a creamery. The old bank in town is now **The Tasting Room.** The restaurants of Carlton are found in this vicinity, too. At **Cuvee,** local foods are used to make French-inspired dishes, pairing them with local wines. For something lighter, **The Horse Radish** is a wine and cheese bar with an extensive variety of both items.

Another way to visit wineries but without having to do any driving is to contact **Grape Escape Tours** and see what Joinable Tours are available during your visit. This group preselects the wineries (from small and diverse winemakers) for groups and you join in the fun. They also have private tours that let you choose the wineries, but those are pricier. You'll want to check with them early, as their tours do fill up quickly.

After staying at the **Abbey Road Farm Bed & Breakfast,** you can return home and let everyone know you slept in a silo. Whether you choose to divulge that the silo has been converted into a fully modern guest room with fine linens and heated towel racks is up to you. The rooms' rounded walls are soothing and the absence of televisions and phones ensure that you are relaxed, too.

The **Trappist Abbey** in Oregon is one of only 12 in the nation.. The monks here are known for their dark fruit cake, which is dipped in good brandy and aged three months. They also make and sell a date nut cake and creamed honey. If you'd like to hike around the monks' 1,300 acres, request a trail map at the abbey's guest house. Retreats and day rooms are available. To get here from Carlton, turn east on Hendricks Road and follow it until going right on Abbey Road.

In Oregon's third-oldest city, Lafayette, you can visit the **Yamhill County Historical Museum,** whose thousands of items take up two buildings.

The first is an 1892 church loaded with pioneer-era items, including doctor's and dentist's equipment, clocks with wooden gears, a doll collection, and even a giant pickle once proudly featured on *Ripley's Believe It or Not.* The second building is the Miller Log Museum, which has an extensive collection of quilts and textiles from the mid-1800s and up, as well as Native American baskets and tools. The town also has its share of antique stores. The **Lafayette Schoolhouse Mall** was built in 1910 and houses about 100

The west side of Henry Hagg Lake is quieter than the east side which allows motorized boats. LAURA STANFILL

dealers. For more modern 1950s collectibles, stop at **The Pack Rat Antique Mall.** For large furniture pieces, check out **Rick's Wholesale Antiques.** Leave town via OR 99 (also called Third Street). Going east will take you to Dayton, or west to McMinnville.

In Dayton's town square you'll find the 1855 Military Blockhouse. Originally at Fort Yamhill, it was moved here in 1911 and has been here since. And if you're wild about wild mushrooms, have dinner at the **Joel Palmer House.** The owners loved hunting for wild mushrooms so much that a restaurant centered on the moisture-loving fungus seemed logical. The restaurant is inside a historic home (1852). Along with the regular menu is Chris's Mushroom Madness Menu. Five of the courses (including meat and fish courses) come with mushrooms, but you are spared having to try them in your dessert. And as is customary for the region, local wines are the specialty. Drink up!

It's hard to pin down McMinnville. In some respects, it's a college town with a small but respected liberal arts college, Linfield (est. 1858). It's also an agricultural town. It's also an artist community and a spot with many treasured historic homes and buildings. The **Evergreen Aviation and Space Museum** is pretty well stocked, considering it's surrounded by agricultural fields. Along with Howard Hughes's *Spruce Goose,* the museum has two Titan missiles with a simulated launch room, a Sea King helicopter, a space shuttle landing simulator, a 3-D IMAX theater, and many more aircraft and space exhibits.

Like much of Oregon, McMinnville is a great spot for bicyclists. There are routes in the Eola Hills among the vineyards, or take the old Sheridan Highway up to the Erratic Rock State Natural Site. Here you'll find a 40-ton rock that was carried here about 15,000 years ago by a glacier, during the prehistoric Missoula floods. A free county-wide bicycling guide is available at the **McMinnville Chamber of Commerce.** If you prefer two feet to two wheels, the **McMinnville Downtown Association** gives walking tours of their historical downtown. Because the downtown (Third Street) is sequestered from the hustling speeds of the highway, it's very pedestrian friendly and full of well-preserved buildings from the days of the gold rush.

Bistro Maison may fool you. You may be enjoying the escargots en croûte, surrounded by warm colors and rich fabrics, and think you've left Oregon for Paris. You haven't. More like Paris has come to you. The husband-and-wife owners were chef and manager at acclaimed New York City restaurants before realizing that Oregon was the place they should be. For breakfast, it's worth the wait to eat at the **Crescent Café.** Just about everything here is homemade, from the sausage to the sticky buns. There's something about a sparkling clean shop like **Honest Chocolates** that harks back to childhood chocolatiers and really lets the candies enjoy the limelight. And these sweets deserve all the attention. Try the chocolates created specifically for wine tastings. They're made with matching wine reduction and fruits paired to your drink. At Honest Chocolates, it's not about ingredients from far-off lands or packaging that screams "expensive." It's about delectable chocolates made by hand and at a reasonable price—the perfect chocolate trifecta.

The end of this trip strategically put you at a spot where you can head west on OR 18 to the central Oregon coast, or east on OR 99, which will take you all the way back to Portland's metro area, your starting point. Of course, I-5 is an easy drive from here, too, and then on to who knows where?

IN THE AREA

Accommodations

Abbey Road Farm Bed & Breakfast, 10275 Northeast Oak Springs Farm Road, Carlton. Call 503-852-6278. Web site: www.abbeyroadfarm .com.

Black Walnut Inn, 9600 Northeast Worden Hill Road, Dundee. Call 503-429-4114 or 1-866-429-4114. Web site: www.blackwalnut-inn.com.

The Carlton Inn, 648 West Main Street, Carlton. Call 503-852-7506 or 1-800-252-6810. Completely restored 1915 home. Web site: www.the carltoninn.com.

Gahr Farm Reserve, 18605 Masonville Road, McMinnville. Call 503-472-6960. Private two-bedroom cottages. Web site: www.gahrfarm.com.

Attractions and Recreation

Carlton Main Street Antiques, 203 West Main Street, Carlton. Call 503-852-0077. Full-size carousel and rocking horses, along with dainty feminine items such as doilies and gloves.

Carlton Winemakers Studio, 750 West Lincoln Street, Carlton. Call 503-852-6100. Taste wine from many smaller producers in one spot. Open daily; closed the month of January. Web site: www.winemakers studio.com.

Cascade Soaring, McMinnville. Call 503-472-7571. Glider rides over wineries, lush farms, and rolling hills.

Cowgirl Mercantile, 448 NE Third Street, McMinnville. Call 503-472-0159. Western clothing and furniture. Web site: www.cowgirlmercantile .com.

Evergreen Aviation & Space Museum, NE Capt. Michael King Smith Way, McMinnville. Call 503-434-4180. *Spruce Goose,* Apollo and Gemini space capsules, and a Titan II missile on display. Web site: www.spruce goose.org.

Grape Escape Tours. Call 503-283-3380. Private and joinable winery tours. Web site: www.grapescapetours.com.

Honest Chocolates, 313 NE Third Street, McMinnville. Call 503-474-9042. It's about the handmade chocolates here, not the fancy boxes and ribbons. Web site: www.honestchocolates.com.

Lafayette Schoolhouse Mall, 748 Third Street, Lafayette. Call 503-864-2720. 100 dealers who sell just about everything from *Life* magazine to Depression glass.

McMinnville Chamber of Commerce, 417 NW Adams Street, McMin-nville. Call 503- 472-6196. Web site: www.mcminnville.org.

McMinnville Downtown Association, 105 NE Third Street, McMin-nville. Call 503-472-3605. Web site: www.downtownmcminnville.com.

Mountainside Lavender, 17805 SW Hillsboro Highway, Hillsboro. Call 503-936-6744. U-pick, gift store, demonstrations. Web site: www .mountainsidelavender.com.

NW Food and Gifts, 445 NE Third Street, McMinnville. Call 503-434-6111. Locally made candles and gourmet food items, and handmade teddy bears.

Stroll through the fields of lavender or learn how to distill the oil at Mountainside Lavender. LAURA STANFILL

Other Contacts

The Pack Rat, 312 Third Street, Lafayette. Call 503-864-3613. Vintage store specializing in 1950s and '60s eras.

The Quilted Hill, 7601 NE Blackburn Road, Yamhill. Call 503-662-4052. One of the top quilt stores in the country. Web site: www.thequiltedhill .com.

RD Steeves Imports, 140 West Main, Yamhill. Call 503-662-3999. Web site: www.rdssteevesimports.com.

Rick's Wholesale Antiques, 780 Third Street, Lafayette. **Call** 503-864-2120. Large furniture pieces imported from England and Europe.

Lunch items and baked goods at South Store Café.   LAURA STANFILL

Scott Paul's Wines, 128 South Pine Street, Carlton. Call 503-852-7300. Web site: wwwscottpaul.com.

Smith Berry Barn, 24500 SW Scholls Ferry Road, Hillsboro. Call 503-628-2172. Fresh produce, gift items, milkshakes, and an espresso bar. Web site: www.smithberrybarn.com.

Trappist Abbey, 9200 NE Abbey Road, Carlton. Call 503-852-0107. Web site: www.trappistabbey.org.

Tyrus Evans Tasting Room, 120 North Pine Street, Carlton. Call 503-852-7010. Located in a historical rail depot.

UFO Festival, McMinnville. Mid-May.

Yamhill County Historical Museum, 605 Market Street, Lafayette. Call 503) 864-2308. Pioneer equipment and quilts. Open Wed., Fri., and Sat. Web site: www.yamhillcountyhistory.org.

Dining/Drinks

Bistro Maison, 729 Northeast Third Street, McMinnville. Call 503-474-1888. Web site: www.bistromaison.com.

Cooper D's, 304 Front Street, Gaston. Call 503-985-0279. A burger joint with good yakisoba as well as bison burgers.

Crescent Café, 526 NE Third Street, McMinnville. Call 503-435-2655. A real breakfast made with care and from scratch.

Cuvee, 214 West Main Street, Carlton. Call 503-852-6278. Closed Mon. and Tues. Web site: www.cuveedining.com.

Filling Station Deli, 305 West Main Street, Carlton. Call 503-852-6687. Picnics to go. Open daily May through Nov.; call for winter hours. Web site: www.fillingstationdeli.com.

The Horse Radish Wine & Cheese Bar, 105 West Main Street, Carlton. Call 503-852-6733. Web site: www.thehorseradish.com.

Joel Palmer House, 600 Ferry Street, Dayton. Call 503-864-2995, Get your fresh fungus here—mushrooms, that is. Closed Mon. Web site: www.joelpalmerhouse.com.

The South Store Café, 24485 SW Scholls Ferry Road, Hillsboro. Call 503-628-1920. Closed Mon.

Zippy's Pizza, 180 South Maple, Yamhill. Call 503-662-3025. Pizza pies and homemade dessert pies. Web site: www.zippyspizza.net.

The grounds at the View Point Inn are vintage in style.
LAURA STANFILL

6

The Old Way Is the Best Way

The Historic Columbia River Highway to Multnomah Falls

Estimated length: 28 miles
Estimated time: 3 hours to 1 day

Getting There: Leave I-84 via exit 17, drive east until SE Kibling, then turn right. Make a left on Historic Columbia River Highway. Continue until after Ainsworth State Park, return to I-84.

Highlights: The Columbia Gorge is part of the Columbia Basin, the third-largest subaerial lava plateau in the world, and includes parts of Idaho and Washington. For these plateaus to form, there must be runny basaltic lava and numerous eruptions, but no violent explosions. This is precisely what happened during a 10- to 15-million-year period, the lava ultimately accumulating 6,000 feet in thickness. Add to this that as the molten rock came up, the earth's crust gradually sank. So what does this all mean for you? It means rivers, lakes, and waterfalls, as well as rich soil that can grow superior fruits and veggies, and remarkable fauna and other flora. Lucky you!

The Columbia River Highway was the first scenic highway constructed in the United States (1913–22). Originally, it was part of the same highway

(OR 30) that extends west to Astoria. As you drive along this panoramic and winding road, imagine the difficulty of traveling on it in bad winter weather or as a trucker hauling freight. In the decades after WWII, the road fell into disrepair. Sections were closed or ignored. The once famous tunnels were demolished, or filled in and bypassed. When I-84 was built, the highway was essentially replaced. Then in the early 1980s, vocal supporters helped to get the highway on the National Register of Historic Places and recognized as a National Historic Civil Engineering Landmark. Now the highway has been restored either for car travel or, farther east, for hiking and bicycling. Along with bridges, parks, and scenic vistas, the highway is best known for the numerous waterfalls that can be seen along the route. And though it isn't necessary to leave your car to see many of them, most are best enjoyed by walking to them. The earlier in the spring or early summer you visit the falls, the more active they are, due to rain and melting snow; however, they are active year-round. It's advisable that you carry a raincoat or poncho if you visit early in the season, as the waterfalls' spray can be heavy.

Public art in Troutdale.   LAURA STANFILL

You can get your pick of candy and other treats at the Troutdale General Store.

Luckily for the town of Troutdale, it's all about location, location, location. When the first sections of the Columbia River Highway were opened in 1916 this was the gateway. Once I-84 moved the traffic away from town, the population started to increase. Now it has the distinction of again being the gateway to the historic highway. The bustling downtown area is mostly made up of tourist-dependent businesses, though a few stalwarts can be seen. You'll find a bit of everything, from Depression glass to Native American pieces, spread out over two floors at **Troutdale Antique Mall.** The 13-foot bronze elk bugling proudly into the sky marks the **Rip Caswell Gallery.** Caswell's work is seen throughout the state at museums, parks, and other institutions. His bronzes come in all sizes and often center on wildlife, frequently with a spiritual emphasis. **Celebrate Me Home** is an unusual mix of espresso bar with sandwiches and quiches in a home furnishings store. **Ristorante Di Pompello** serves sandwiches, as well as

Outside the Rip Caswell Gallery

entrées for lunch and dinner. It's best to stick with their basics. If you're in the area for dinner during the week, a reasonably priced special menu for two is offered there. The traveling crowd and locals gather at the **Trout-dale General Store,** and for good reasons: the "stick to your ribs" baked oatmeal squares with peaches and cinnamon for breakfast, and for lunch the Cajun meatloaf sandwich. A majority of the seating is upstairs, which has a nice deck. They also carry chocolates from Portland phenomenon, Moonstruck Chocolates. And since no Oregon small town would be complete without a railroad-inspired attraction, Troutdale's **Rail Depot Museum** (1882) is small but the caboose out front is open to the public, too.

As you leave Troutdale, the historic highway is to the right, but a turn to the left will take you to the **Lewis and Clark State Recreation Area.** Along most of this section of the Lewis and Clark Expedition, the duo and crew camped on what is now the Washington side of the Columbia River. However, in November 1805, they camped not far from here. A couple of hiking trails meander through trees believed to be roughly 700 years old. A steep trail leads to Broughton's Bluff, a popular spot for local rock climbers. There's also interpretive signage detailing the plants used by Lewis and Clark either as food or medicinally.

As you start to follow the highway again, mimicking the curves of the Sandy River, you'll come to **Tad's Chicken 'n Dumplings** on the right. Around since the 1930s, the restaurant has had different owners over the decades but the chicken and dumplings have always remained on the menu. If you're looking for a place to wow you with chic modern décor and artfully drizzled sauces, then it's best to drive past. The walls are covered in knotty pine panels and there is an amalgamation of vintage knickknacks and tchotchkes on all three stories. The restaurant is open for dinner only and does have a full menu of non-dumpling-related choices. Next is **Dabney State Recreation Area.** Popular with nearby residents, it features picnic facilities, a swimming spot, and an 18-hole disc golf course.

Art communities are pervasive in Oregon but not all of them are as charming or affable as Springdale's. The Springdale School Community Association houses the **Springdale School Art Network.** The historic school is well worth a stop, though who's available and what's open is up to chance. The old classrooms house different artist studios, some sharing. It's very un-gallery-like, with no stuffiness or strategic lighting. If you're interested in buying art directly from the artist, this is the place.

Eight miles farther is the town of Corbett and the **View Point Inn.** Many small notable inns use similar Victorian décor throughout their property. Thankfully, the four rooms at the View Point Inn do not. They're lavish, posh, and soothing, not layered with flouncy linens or an over-abundance of patterned period wallpapers. The inn was originally opened in 1925 and is the only building on this highway that's on the National Reg-

The Sandy River just east of Troutdale   LAURA STANFILL

ister of Historic Places but isn't government owned or operated. In its original heyday, big-name visitors to the Columbia Gorge stayed here: Charlie Chaplin, Franklin Roosevelt, and Clara Bow, to name a few. If that isn't impressive, how about that the inn was used for the prom scene in the first *Twilight* movie? If you're not staying at the inn, you'll still want to eat in the restaurant. It has the same view, the same history, and the same regal aura as the rest of the inn and is bigger than you'd expect from a lodging property with only four rooms. The restaurant uses a seasonal menu and if the Sweet Onion and Saffron Soup is available, order it. Sunday brunch here is your best bet, but expect a wait. Try the mascarpone-stuffed French toast or house-made corned beef hash. If some light libations and cocktails are needed, head to the lounge housed in what used to be the garage. There are fire pits and outdoor seating just for the lounge guests, and that same gorgeous view.

Many photos of the Columbia Gorge seen in print were quite possibly taken at the **Women's Forum Outlook.** Why don't you stop and take your own photo? The view here is splendid. This is also a good spot to put yourself in the shoes of the Oregon Trail pioneers. Until later, when Samuel Barlow and his Barlow Toll Road took them around the south side of Mount Hood, the wagons had to be put atop rafts and floated down the Columbia River to reach Oregon City. This would happen east of here around the towns of The Dalles and Rowena. They were so close to their final destination and still the crossing was fraught with danger.

The 14-mile offshoot to Larch Mountain and **Sherrard View Point** is absolutely worth the detour. The volcanic peak sits at 4,055 feet high and was named after a fir tree in the area, marketed as "larch." During the late summer and early fall, a little bit of inspection might turn up the elusive huckleberries. Because the berries have never been cultivated commercially, this is a real treat. Just be sure to pick only what you plan to eat, as the fruit doesn't hold up well. From here, Multnomah Creek flows north to become Multnomah Falls, which you'll be seeing soon. What makes this 28-mile round trip a gem is the exceptional views of mountains Saint Helens, Rainier, Adams, Hood, and Jefferson. There are picnic tables as well. This dining al fresco might be the best in the state. Be aware that the road

The View Point Inn in Corbett.   LAURA STANFILL

Inside the Crown Point Vista House. LAURA STANFILL

closes with the first snowfall and usually opens by June. The weather can be breezier and cooler up here, too.

Moving from one astonishing view to another, once you return to the highway you'll reach illustrious **Crown Point Vista House,** perched 733 feet above the Columbia River. Originally completed in 1918 for $100,000, this illustrious building was intended as a spot for weary travelers to enjoy the highest spot on the drive and, according to highway design engineer Samuel Lancaster, the "view both up and down the Columbia could be viewed in silent communion with the infinite." The architect responsible for the instantly recognizable building, Edgar Lazarus, was the brother of Emma Lazarus, the woman responsible for penning the poem the words, "Give me your tired, your poor . . ." were taken from. The foundation was built without cement and mortar by Italian craftsmen. Inside are floors and walls of rare Alaskan marble. There are four sets of unidentified Indian busts facing each other in mirror image, for a total of eight. Stone carvings inside the house honor Oregon's pioneers who were influential in making the state what it is today: a newspaper publisher and printer, library founder and university regent, first territorial governor, and Fort Vancouver's chief factor. Over time, the building has been wracked by the wet, windy, and cold weather. For four years, the structure was closed for renovations, inside and out, at a cost of 3.2 million dollars.

The view from atop the Crown Point Vista House.   LAURA STANFILL

To see Latourell Falls, park at the **Guy W. Talbot State Park.** This picturesque spot was once the Talbot family's summer home until it was donated to the city. The trail to the falls takes you under the highway. Plunging 249 feet, the falls have a sweet footbridge in front and are surrounded by mossy rocks. Keep going past the lower falls another ¾ mile to the upper falls. Although they are shorter, you can get behind these latter falls. Back on the highway and just a mile farther is **Shepperd's Dell State Natural Area.** The land was given as part of the highway to the public in 1915 by George Shepperd in memory of his wife. This land had nostalgic importance to him because before the highway, the Shepperd family visited here on Sundays when getting to church was impossible without a road. At the east end of the bridge are stairs and a trail leading to the Shepperd's Dell Falls.

There are two trails at Bridal Veil Falls. The upper trail has informative signage about the native plants here. This trail is wheelchair accessible and takes you to some wonderful gorge views, including the Pillars of Hercules. The lower trail takes you to the base of Bridal Veil Falls and is about a mile there and back. This one is a little steep, not wheelchair accessible, and, depending on the season, can be very muddy. Be sure not to stray from the trail or you may encounter poison ivy. Taking the bridge to see the falls is tempting but it is a narrow two-lane road and has no sidewalk. Sadly, the logging community of Bridal Veil is all gone. The hope of the Crown Point Country Historical Society was to make its buildings a museum devoted the area's logging past, but they lost the battle with the Trust for Public Land and the structures were destroyed. However, along with the cemetery, there is still a post office dating from around 1887. Why a post office but no community? The postmark from Bridal Veil is coveted for wedding invitations. Come early spring, the post office receives thousands of envelopes to be hand canceled with the name. This has kept the post office from being permanently closed. If it's open and you'd like to support the efforts to keep Bridal Veil from being wiped from the maps, purchase some stamps.

Wahkeena Falls cascades for 242 feet and is said to be named for the Yakima tribe's word for "most beautiful." This is another waterfall that can be seen from the highway and the view is nice, but a short hike from the parking lot is rewarded with a footbridge located at the base of the upper falls. The hike can continue, if you're up to it, to Fairy Falls, but it does get steep for the next ½ mile. If you do that, you'll have to walk all the way back

Multnomah Falls. LAURA STANFILL

to your car parked at Wahkeena Falls. Instead, descend and drive down I-84 to Mutnomah.

Now you've arrived at Multnomah Falls. This waterfall beauty queen has been the public face of Oregon for a century or so. And no matter how many pictures you've seen, none compares to seeing her in person. Because this fall is so easily accessed from I-84, it can get crowded here. Parking is a bit wacky and folks are always jostling to take photos. It's like being among natural wonders' paparazzi. But all the folks who just took a single exit to get here missed all the abovementioned majestic marvels you've just witnessed. Before heading up to the Benson Footbridge (1914), check inside at the information area. The opening of the highway to this point was a big deal. In 1916, 10,000 people showed up for the dedication ceremonies. The Multnomah Falls Lodge's architect, A. E. Doyle, is famous in Portland and also designed the famed Benson Hotel, the county's central library, and the Meier & Frank Department Store. The original lodge was constructed in 1925 for just $40,000 and has had at least two additions built onto it.

The poetic Columbia Highway design engineer, Samuel Lancaster, wrote of Multnomah Falls, "It charms like magic, it woos like an ardent lover; it refreshes the soul; and invites to loftier, purer things." While few things say Oregon like Multnomah Falls, no one is sure where that name comes from. There's talk of an Indian tale about a selfless woman's throwing herself over them for her tribe, but that was most likely created by pioneers. Meriwether Lewis and other 19-century explorers mentioned the falls in their journals, but gave them no name. Although many of the spots they passed were already named by the native tribes, still the newcomers named landmarks after their bosses, themselves, their preferred saint, childhood home, and so on. There was no Chief Multnomah, or anyone else with that name.

The next falls are about 2.5 miles farther down the highway: Oneonta Falls. This is a more difficult hike due to slippery rocks, and has the prospect of your getting wet in chilly Oneonta Creek. Round trip, the hike is about a mile and is best done on hot days. Sorry, but this one is not viewable from the road. Just ½ mile from the last waterfall parking lot is another waterfall that can't be seen from the car. Horsetail Falls tumbles 176 feet to a refreshing (albeit cold) swimming hole. From here, a steep 1.3-mile trail to Ponytail Falls starts. This trail enters a cave directly below and behind the falls. Watch for slippery rocks. Farther up, a phenomenal view of Oneonta Gorge can be seen from a footbridge. The entire loop trail is just under 3 miles. Continuing east on Columbia Highway, past Ainsworth State Park, will return you to I-84.

What happened to all the green? And all the trees? If you're continuing on I-84 east, the average rainfall decreases about an inch for every mile you go from Cascade Locks to The Dalles. At the Oneonta Falls, annual rainfall averages about 75 inches a year. East of The Dalles Dam, it's about 12 inches. Snow at the river level is rare, but on top of Mount Hood it can total 430 inches. No one can say Oregon isn't full of extremes.

If you've come to the end of this trip with time to spare, get back on I-84 and head east. There's so much more Columbia Gorge exploring to do: Bonneville Dam (17 miles); Eagle Creek; trips on the Sternwheeler river ship; more waterfalls; and Hood River's restaurants, shops, and galleries (40 miles). And that's just the beginning.

The following destinations are for those heading back west toward I-5, Willamette Valley, Portland, the coast, and so on. This is because they are on the north side of I-84 and parallel to where you have just come from. **Benson State Recreation Area** is best known for its lake's being freshly stocked each month with thousands of rainbow trout. Each year, around the first weekend in June, is Free Fishing Day. They provide everything you need to fish, even equipment. But if you've had your share of exercise today with all the hiking to waterfalls, why not watch someone else do the hard work for a bit? On a windy day at **Rooster Rock State Park,** you can lie on the grass and watch windsurfers catch air. The Columbia Gorge is known throughout the world as a prime windsurfing locale. The park has 3 miles of beach for strolling and sunbathing. Be aware that at the far eastern end is an official nude beach (one of two in the state), but it is purposely separated and can't be viewed from the clothing-required beach. In fall, the maple and oaks at the east end of the park spark with the season's flaming colors and provide a beautiful backdrop for a stroll. And there are not one but two disc golf courses here; the one to the east is the more challenging course. The park has easy on and off freeway access (exit 25) and has a designated off-leash area for dogs. There is no camping or RVs at either park.

IN THE AREA

Accommodations

Ainsworth State Park, 4 miles from Multnomah Falls, exit 35 of I-84. Call 503-695-2301 or 503-695-2261. RV and tent sites. Open mid-Mar. through Oct. Web site: www.oregonparks.org.

Brickhaven Bed and Breakfast, 38717 East Columbia River Highway, Corbett. Call 503-695-5126. Outstanding views; a stay includes a full country breakfast. Web site: www.brickhaven.com.

Cedarplace Inn Bed & Breakfast, 2611 South Troutdale Road, Troutdale. Call 503-491-1900 or 1-877-491-1907. Web site: www.cedarplc inn.com.

Columbia Gorge RV Village, 633 East Historic Columbia River Highway, Troutdale. Call 503-665-6722.

Crown Point RV Park, 37000 East Columbia River Highway, Corbett. Call 503-695-5207. Tent and RV spaces.

McMenamins Edgefield, 2126 SW Halsey Street, Troutdale. Call 503-669-8610. Massage, winery, live music, movie theaters, and gardens sitting on more than 35 acres. Web site: www.mcmenamins.com.

Sandy River Front RV Resort, 633 East Historic Columbia River Highway, Troutdale. Call 503-665-6722.

Viewpoint Inn, 40301 East Larch Mountain Road, Corbett. Call 503-695-5811. A historic home, now an inn, with four rooms, a large, fine restaurant, and remarkable views.

Attractions and Recreation

Benson Lake State Park, off I-84, exit 30. Features a motorboat-free lake stocked with thousands of trout each month. Web site: www.oregon stateparks.org.

Bev Frank Antiques, 387 East Columbia River Highway, Troutdale. Call 503-665-1640.

Caswell Gallery, 101 West Columbia Highway, Troutdale. Call 503-492-2473. Bronzes of all sizes, many of area wildlife. Web site: www.ripcaswell.com.

Corbett Country Market, 36801 East Historic Columbia Highway, Corbett. Call 503-695-2234. The only gas station between Troutdale and Cascade Locks. Pick up some local jerky here, too.

Rail Depot Museum, 473 East Historic Columbia River Highway, Troutdale. Call 503-661-2164. Open Tues. through Fri. Web site: www.troutdale history.org.

River Trails. Call 503-667-1964. Kayak, canoe, and raft lessons. www.nwrivertrails.com.

Rooster Rock Sternwheeler Columbia Gorge, exit 44 off I-84, Cascade Locks. Call 541-374-8427 or 1-800-643-1354. Web site: www.sternwheeler.com.

Springdale School Art Network, 32405 East Historic Columbia River Highway, Springdale. Call 503-695-6070. Local artists and their studios. Web site: www.springdaleartnetwork.com.

Troutdale Antique Mall, 359 East Columbia River Highway, Troutdale. Call 503-674-6820.

Vista House at Crown Point, 40700 East Historic Columbia River Highway, a few miles from Corbett. Call 503-695-2230. Open daily, mid-Mar. to Oct., for no fee. Web site: www.vistahouse.com.

Dining/Drinks

Black Rabbit Restaurant and Bar, 2126 SW Halsey, Troutdale. Call 503-492-3086. Breakfast, lunch, dinner, and handcrafted ales in a casual atmosphere. Not for recommended for diners in a rush, but the food is enjoyable. Web site: www.mcmenamins.com.

Celebrate Me Home, 319 East Columbia River Highway, Troutdale. Call 503-618-9394. Espresso bar and snacks inside a home furnishings store.

The work of local artists can be found at the Springdale School Art Network.

Ristorante Di Pompello, 177 East Historic Columbia River Highway, Troutdale. Call 503-667-2480. Serving Italian food for lunch and dinner.

Tad's Chicken 'n Dumplings, 1325 East Columbia River Highway, Troutdale. Call 503-666-5337. On weekends and in the summer, this place can get busy. The earlier or later you arrive, the better your chance of a shorter wait. Web site: www.tadschicdump.com.

Troutdale General Store, 289 East Columbia River Highway, Troutdale. Call 503-492-7912. Open breakfast, lunch and dinner. Inside are a candy store, wine shop, gift shop, and antique soda fountain.

Other Contacts

Forest Service, Columbia River Gorge, 902 Wasco Street, Suite 200, Hood River. Call 541-308-1700. Web site: www.fs.fed.us.

One of Oregon's many lovely and graceful bridges.

CHAPTER

7

Fields of Gold and Relics

Northern Central Oregon

Estimated length: 165 miles
Estimated time: 5 hours to 2 days

Getting There: From either direction on US 84, I-97 can be found at the same exit as the town of Biggs. Take I-97 south to the town of Antelope. From Antelope, take OR 218 east to Fossil. At Fossil, take OR 19 north to Condon. OR 19 joins back up with US 84.

Highlights: Head into the Oregon of wheat and barley farming, fossils, and hearty pioneers. Taking I-97 south leaves the dense forest and trees behind and directs you to where life was hard but rewards were possible. This road is about valleys and vistas, with few other travelers on the same road. The first half of this trip is located in Sherman County, which has more square miles under cultivation than any other county in Oregon. The trip's other half is in Gilliam County, the heart of the Columbia Plateau's wheat area: the quiet town of **Wasco,** an informative **Moro,** the welcoming **Grass Valley,** the almost ghost town of **Shaniko,** the mysterious past of **Antelope,** fossil spotting at the **Clarno Unit** of John Day Fossil Beds as well as in **Fossil,** and a restful stopover in **Condon.** Then it's on past the modern windmills to **Arlington.**

Earl Snell Memorial Park located in Arlington

Nine miles in on I-97 (completed in 1925) is the town of **Wasco**. The name is derived from a tribe of Chinook Indians that lived on the south side of the Columbia River. Here the original **Columbia Southern Railway Depot** (1898) is now the Wasco Railroad and City Historical Center. The building is on the National Register of Historic Places. The park that houses the building also has a caboose to explore, along with a children's play area and small skateboard course. The town has limited accommodations: the **Just Us Inn,** which appears to have lots of color and character but is short on amenities and upkeep, was at the time of this writing, up for sale.

Once in town, look for signs for the **Oregon Trail interpretive kiosk** from the Bureau of Land Management and the Sherman County Historical Society. The kiosk is less than 5 miles east of town. Picnic tables are available.

A tranquil spot for picnicking or stretching is **DeMoss Springs,** 6 six miles south of Wasco. The grounds are kept up nicely and there are restroom facilities. The land originally belonged to James M. DeMoss, a United Brethren minister and his family. He, his wife, and their eldest son crossed the Oregon Trail in 1862. The couple were musically inclined and passed on this talent to their five children. While touring as the DeMoss

Lyric Bards, they camped on this spot and decided to purchase it. They would go on to tour domestically and abroad until 1933.

Moro is a sweet, sleepy small town, home to antique shops, galleries, and the award-winning **Sherman County Historical Museum.** This stop is a must for any traveler interested in Native American artifacts, the Oregon Trail, farming and livestock methods of previous eras, railroads, or rural life from horsepower to steam engines. To engage children in the history, the museum's art projects include rubbings based on local pictographs and

An authentic chuck wagon on display at the Sherman County Historical Museum.

Tractors just get more attractive with age.

petroglyphs. But before they get their hands dirty, encourage the kids to try on the reproductions of pioneer clothing. The museum also has a pleasant children's park located next to it. Like most small towns not on the well-traveled path, the hours and days of operation for the local businesses aren't always posted and can get creative. But the walk down Main Street of Moro (or any other town) offers chances to see things you might have missed by simply driving through. Or the chance to partake in something rare in the cities: a pleasant conversation with a stranger about any number of subjects.

Stopping in Grass Valley, just 10 miles south on US 97, is suggested if you're looking for a bite to eat. The **Grass Valley Country Market** serves freshly made sandwiches and other deli items. The menu can be a bit limited after a busy weekend, but Jim and Carol are friendly and don't make your items until ordered. The phrase "eat off the floor" never rang more true than it does at this establishment. Not only is the place spic-and-span, the husband-and-wife owners lovingly refurbished the original (1903) fir floors, taking off four back-breaking layers of finish. This is a place where the regulars are known by name. Grass Valley also has a small grocery store that carries basic staples, liquor, and things like motor oil and charcoal briquettes. Auto racing lovers may want to head 2 miles east of town to check out the **Oregon Raceway Park.** If the timing is right (usually weekends), there might be sports bike or Porsche racing. The gas station in Grass Valley is the only one until Fossil.

Past Kent, the next town, at mile marker 53 is the infamous **Shoe Tree** that defies logic and explanation. Why would folks toss athletic shoes, tied at the laces, up into a large dead tree? Is it a tradition signifying a rite of passage or just a way to prove that tourists will stop at anything? Whatever the reason, it's entertaining and humorous. As you approach, the tree will shimmer in the sun like a Christmas tree laden with garlands and Mylar icicles. There is a turnout for parking, though it is best suited for autos and not RVs.

The ghost town of **Shaniko** comes up very quickly on your left. It's a funny little tourist attraction that's worth the stop. But because roughly 30 people still call Shaniko home, it's not quite a ghost town. It was named for August Scherneckau, a pioneer who originally settled the area and became its first postmaster in 1879, when it was known as Cross Hollows due to its topography. The town was planned and built by busi-

The almost ghost town of Shaniko.

The shoe tree outside of Shaniko needs no explanation.

nessmen and incorporated in 1901. The main cash crop was sheep's wool roving. By 1911, the train traffic was diverted and Shaniko began to decline. Many buildings remain and some have been restored and are open to the public. The residents of and around Shaniko have tried valiantly to save their history and still offer something interesting and fun for road trippers. Sadly, an enterprising Oregon businessman purchased much of the town and then argued with them about water rights. Lodging can be found at the restored **Shaniko Hotel and Café**—built in 1900—but it's best to call ahead. Once you've pulled into town, visit **Goldie's Ice Cream.** The old-time parlor carries ice cream made in nearby Redmond.

As you leave Shaniko, you'll want to head south out of town (leaving from Goldie's Ice Cream, make a left) toward Antelope and OR 218. The "sneeze and you might miss it" joke truly applies to the town of **Antelope,** just 8 miles from Shaniko. But a few of those miles are on a preposterously crooked road that leads the eye to stunning views of the valley below. The sign at the edge of town reads, POPULATION 37, but this tiny town has an unusual recent history. The post office was established in 1871 and all was pretty quiet until the 1980s, when the followers of Bhagwan Shree Rajneesh moved into the area. The commune at the former Big Muddy Ranch grew to 4,000 followers and in September 1984, the town's charter was amended to change the name from Antelope to Rajneesh by a vote of 57 to 22. In 1984, members of the commune deliberately introduced salmonella organisms into salad bars at restaurants in The Dalles and 750 people were taken sick. Then the Bhagwan's secretary absconded with much of the sect's funds. The Bhagwan returned to India guilty of federal immigration charges. In November 1985, the vote was unanimous to change the name back to Antelope. It's possible that reading this short history took longer to get through than driving through Antelope does. There is a plaque dedicated to the residents who stayed and resisted the "invasion and occupation." As you leave town, the OR 218 veers left.

Oregon's version of the "crookedest street"

This trip goes through two counties, Sherman and Gilliam, separated by the John Day River. While the river is well known to fisherman, its namesake is not. The Astor-Hunt expedition left Saint Louis in 1810, with setting up a post at the mouth of the Columbia as its goal. However, the group suffered from differing opinions and divided. John Day's group dwindled to just two, due to extreme hardships. Close to the mouth of the river that would eventually be named after him, the survivors were attacked by Indians who took everything, including their clothes. Although the men were rescued, some sources say they went insane and died in 1814.

About 25 miles farther down the crooked road is the **Clarno Unit** of the **John Day Fossil Beds National Monument.** The cliffs of the **Palisades** are first from this direction. Formed 44 million years ago by volcanic mudflows called lahars, the Palisades preserved many fossils back when the area was a forest fed by 100 inches of rain a year. Two trails, each ¼ mile long, start here. The Trail of the Fossils leads to easily viewed imbedded fossils. The Clarno Arch trail has a moderate climb that takes you directly to a natural arch in the cliffs. Petrified logs can also be seen in the face of the cliffs. A lovely picnic area can be found about ¼ mile down OR 218. The Geologic Time Trail leads ¼ mile from the picnic area to the trails mentioned above, with signs that note prehistoric events of the past 50 million years. Please don't remove fossils, as they are protected at all of the three John Day units.

The county courthouse in Fossil.

The pleasing town of **Fossil** is just 8 miles farther on OR 218. By now, you'll be itching to try some hunting of your own fossils. Behind

The Clarno Unit of the John Day Fossil Beds.

the Wheeler High School football field (April through October), is the only public fossil field in the United States. Just bring your own tools (a small shovel or garden trowel, gloves, etc.) and dig away to your heart's content. The tools aren't completely necessary. as often the fossils can be found by just turning rocks over. However, as you leave, someone will ask to check out what you've found. Should a fossil be rare or unidentifiable, then it must be given to the on-site collection. If it's a new species, your name will be added to the scientific name. Then, you will be allowed to leave with your three choicest fossils. Recently the town has added a gift shop, restrooms, and a knowledgeable docent to answer questions.

Now that the dirt has left you parched, grab a cool drink from **Fossil Mercantile.** New and vintage quilts, fabric and grocery items are available. This is the sole grocery store in town and has been in business since 1883. A 15-foot-tall iron sculpture of a wooly mammoth can be found on Main Street, in front of Fossil Lodge. And for a more recent history of the area, visit the one-room Pine Creek Schoolhouse Museum and the Fossil Museum, the latter of which has the window from the original town post office.

In the summer, this drive can get pretty warm and searching for fossils can make you wish for shade. **Dyer State Wayside,** located approximately 4 miles north of Fossil, has just what you need: locust and fruit trees, along with picnic tables and restrooms.

About 15 miles north is **Condon,** a town that seems like a trip back in time. The area was first settled as Summit Springs, due to a freshwater spring used by sheep herders. As in most of this part of Oregon, the early residents decided to start growing wheat. By the early 1900s, Condon was known as "Wheat City," for shipping more of the grain than any other city its size. Given its present a population of less than 800, it's satisfying to know that not one but two Nobel Prize winners spent their childhood here: Linus Pauling (1954 Chemistry and 1962 Peace) and William Parry Murphy (1934 Medicine).

The town's Americana look isn't just for show; it's the real thing. As you enter Condon from the south, you'll pass their well-maintained and picturesque city park. Across the street is the **Twist & Shake,** a swell place to grab a burger. Each August, the Condon Cruise into History fills the town's streets with vintage cars, motorcycles, and trucks.

Many of the building on Main Street are registered as Historic Sites. Several have been restored, and there are plans to do the same for the rest. One of these is the **Hotel Condon,** which has been completely refurbished with many modern hotel details yet has kept its innate charm. The hotel was originally built in 1920 and has 18 guest rooms, including some suites, and is surprisingly posh for such a remote location. Although everything from the décor and comfy beds to the complimentary wireless connections has been updated, there are no stuffy attitudes here. Burgers and the basics are great, but at some point on your trip, treat yourself to a lovely dinner. The **Sage Restaurant,** located inside the hotel, makes almost every menu item on the premises. The bread, dressings, and desserts rank as some of the best for miles. Hopefully, the main dining room will be open for you. Eating in the lounge is acceptable, just not as vintage or glamorously decorated. The prices are a bit high for the area, but not for the quality or quantity of the food.

Directly across the street is **Country Flowers,** an enchanting store complete with a soda fountain and coffee bar, a cowboy-themed reading room, and a one-room annex of Powell's—Portland's famous bookstore. Along with being the local flower shop, the store is stocked with knick-knacks and tools for the garden, kitchen, and country-décor home. The building dates from 1905 and many of the display cases are from the occupying businesses of the past decades. (The original cash register is beauti-

The Hotel Condon balances modern amenities with small-town friendliness.

fully crafted but can only ring up to $9.99.) The town also has a first-run single-screen movie theater whose film is run only once a day, usually at 7 PM.

From here, OR 19 becomes a winding and solitary road almost all of the 40 miles to **Arlington.** Along with the wind turbines using the plentiful gusts and breezes of the area, an Oregon Trail Historic Marker can be found shortly after the road leading to Mikkalo. It comes up on the left, and the curve in the road can make it easy to miss. As you near Arlington, **China Creek,** a newer (2003) inexpensive golf course, is on the left. This is a nine-hole course with bluffs overlooking the river. The small town (population 524) boasts three parks and plenty of water for aquatic sport lovers. The most accessible park is **Earl Snell Memorial Park,** located right on the Columbia River, and has a lagoon for swimming. If the weather cooperates, take along your meal from the **Pheasant Grill** just a block before the park. Or if you're not that hungry, at least get one of their handmade shakes. Each day, they feature a made-from-scratch special. Lucky travelers will come to town when salmon is on that day's menu. Now you're back at US 84, just 35 miles east of where you originally left it.

Most the towns on this trip are trying hard to make your visit as pleasant, relaxing, and ideal as you hoped. There are some Oregonians who have never visited them and don't know what peace and tranquility they offer. After completing this journey, you've visited towns smaller than most big-city high schools. Hopefully, you've come away with a new appreciation for those who tilled the first fields and built the first homes. Their hard work and the work of their modern counterparts deserve our admiration.

IN THE AREA

Accommodations

Bear Hollow Campground Park, 42853 Highway 19, Fossil. 5 miles south of Fossil on OR 19. Potable water and restrooms. Open Apr. through Oct.

Bridge Creek Flora Inn, 828 Main Street, Fossil. Call 541-763-2355. 12 rooms between the inn and lodge. Includes an all-you-can-eat breakfast. Web site: www.fossilinn.com.

Always keep an eye out for interesting historical markers.

Hotel Condon, 202 South Main Street, Condon. Call 541-384-4624 or 1-800-201-6706. A completely renovated 1920 hotel with complimentary WiFi. www.hotelcondon.com.

Port of Arlington RV Park, Arlington Park Rd. and the Columbia River. Call 541-454-2868. No reservations. Open Apr. through Oct. Full hook-up sites available. Web site: www.honkernet.net.

Shelton Park, 7 miles south of Fossil on OR 19. Call 541-763-2400. Potable water and restrooms.

Sherman County RV Park, 66147 Lonerock Road, Moro. Call 541-565-3127. Take Highway 97 to the center of Moro. Turn east at the Fairgrounds sign, then it's about a mile to the RV park adjacent to the fairgrounds. Enter at the upper gate.

Tall Winds Motel, 301 Main St, Moro. Call 541-565-3519. Open year-round.

Wilson Ranches Retreat, 16555 Butte Creek Road, Fossil. Call 541-763-2227 or 1-866-763-2227. A dude ranch that is also a working cattle ranch, located 2 miles west of town. Web site: www.wilsonranchesretreat.com.

Attractions and Recreation

China Creek Golf Course, Highway 19 South. Call 541-454-2000. The course features 2,627 yards of golf from the longest tees for a par of 34. The hilly course can be strenuous if you're walking. Open year-round. Web site: www.honkernet.net.

Country Flowers, 201 South Main Street, Condon. Call 541-384-4120. Country gift store with items for every room of the home. Small deli and coffee bar. Powell's Books annex. Web site: www.countryflowerscondon .com

Fossil Bed at Wheeler High School, East B Street, Fossil. Call 541-763-4146. An inexpensive and unusual activity. Children six and under are free.

Fossil Museum, 501 First Street, Fossil. Call 541-763-2113. Open daily, Memorial Day through Labor Day.

Harvest Moon Gallery, 408 Main Street, Moro. Call 541-565-0500. Local fine arts and crafts.

Liberty Theater, 212 South Main Street, Condon. Call 541-384-2120. One screening each evening of first-run movies.

Moro Now & Then, 405 North Main Street, Moro. Call 541-565-0553. From dollhouse accessories to baseball trading cards.

Oregon Raceway Park, 93811 Blagg Lane, Grass Valley, 2 miles east on North Road. Call 541-333-0810. Races are mostly on weekends. Check the Web site or call for the racing schedule. Web site: www.oregonrace way.com.

Paleo Lands Bookshop and Gallery, 401 Fourth Street, Fossil. Call 541-763-4480. A WiFi coffeehouse that carries Oregon and paleontology books. Hiking maps and local art available.

Paleo Lands Field Center, 333 Fourth Street, Fossil. Call 541-763-4480. Stop for maps, guides, and travel advice, all geared toward area fossil beds. Web site: www.paleolands.org.

Sherman County Historical Museum, 200 Dewey Street, Moro. Call 541-565-3232. More than 15,000 artifacts, including Oregon Trail and Native American. Open daily, May through Oct. Web site: www.sherman museum.org.

Sweet Memories of Moro, 101 Main Street, Moro. Call 541-565-3556. An antique store in the historic Moro Hotel.

Dining

Antelope Store and Café, Main and Union Streets, Antelope. The burgers are made with local beef, and the marionberry cobbler and shakes are wonderful. Call 541-489-3413.

Café Moro, 410 Main Street, Highway 97, Moro. Call 541-565-3716. Irregular hours.

Grass Valley Market, 104 North Mill Street, Grass Valley. Call 541-333-2507. Deli and market open daily. Web site: www.grassvalleycountry market.com.

Lean-To Café, 13 Clark Street #A, Wasco. Call 541-442-5709.

Pheasant Grill, 300 Locust, Arlington. Call 541-454-2712. Dine in and take out. Daily specials. Lunch and dinner.

The classic neon sign of the Pheasant Grill in Arlington.

Sage Restaurant, 202 South Main Street, Condon; Call 541-384-4624 or 1-800-201-6706. Web site: www.hotelcondon.com.

Twist & Shake, 433 South Main Street, Condon. Call 541-384-3922. '50s style burger joint. Open daily, breakfast through dinner.

CHAPTER

8

The Road with Less Travelers

Eastern Oregon's Elkhorn Scenic Byway

Estimated length: 105 miles
Estimated time: 5 hours to 1 full day

Getting There: Be aware that once you start the Elkhorn Scenic Byway, there isn't a gas station for the first 57 miles. While you are on the byway, gas can only be bought in the towns of Granite and Sumpter—so consider filling the tank in North Powder or Haines before getting started. Leave I-84 at exit 285 and head west. Go left on Ellis Road, then right on Anthony Lake Road (FR 53). Follow this byway to Anthony and LaGrande Lakes. At junction with FR 73, head left. After Sumpter, this road merges with OR 7. Continue on this highway until Baker City. Due to snow, the road from Anthony Lake to Granite is usually closed until July 4. However, the byway up to the Anthony Lakes Ski Resort and from Granite to Baker City can be accessed in winter. Check road conditions first.

Highlights: The good news is, Americans are getting out and familiarizing themselves with their expansive nation. The bad news is, they're on the same road you are. Some days, getting away from it all puts you smack dab in the middle of everybody looking to do the same. The loveliest spots can be the busiest. But, the Elkhorn Scenic Byway offers quiet solitude without your leaving paved roads. Most of this byway is located in the Wallowa-Whitman Forest, the largest in the northwest at more than 2.3 million acres. Most of this byway is located in the Wallowa-Whitman Forest, the largest in the northwest at more than 2.3 million acres. How is it that so many miss this relaxing, meandering, interesting byway? No idea, but good for those who venture out onto its asphalt.

Right after you exit I-84, a quick detour from this byway will take you to the **John W. McKean Wildlife Viewing Area.** The chance of seeing a herd of elk is greater during the winter, when they come down from the snowy mountains. If you want to get really close, **T&T Wildlife Tours** can take you on Oregon's only horse-drawn-wagon elk tour. The herd tends to be about 250 head. This group is staffed by experts who will fill you in on their mission and duties in caring for the land and the animals. They've been doing so for nearly two decades. The ride is very family friendly and the wagon is accessible to wheelchairs. Follow WILDLIFE VIEWING AREA signs and arrows for 4 miles.

OR 53 is a winding road that climbs higher and higher. Once you reach the Baker Valley Overlook on your left, you can see where you've come from. Not only did you leave the lower elevation behind, but in the warmer months the heat, too. The valley can get pretty warm in the late summer. On a good clear day, you can see the peaks of Eagle Cap Wilderness straight ahead.

One of the country's first ski slopes (1933), **Anthony Lake Ski Area** comes up on your left about 5 miles after the overlook. After the access road was rebuilt in 1936, one of country's first rope ski tows was created, thanks to the dedicated local ski club. Later on, the local ski patrol was part of the organizing of the National Ski Patrol. They claim to have the highest base elevation (7,100 feet) in Oregon.

About 20 miles into the Elkhorn Scenic Byway is **Anthony Lake,** a peaceful alpine lake also at a 7,100-foot elevation. The driveway for the **Anthony Lake Campground** is on your left. At the fork in the road, turn to your right for the day-use area, which includes picnic tables and a gazebo with a rock fireplace. There are plenty of places to just sit, dip your feet in the lake, and enjoy the quiet. Or for a more active stay, the Hoffer Lakes

Anthony Lake and Gunsight Mountain.

Interpretive Trail is a 1-mile easy walk around the lake. Anthony Lake was produced by a glacier—recently, by geological standards: somewhere between 6,000 and 10,000 years ago. Overlooking the lake (directly across from the gazebo) is Gunsight Mountain. At 8,342 feet, it looks like, well, a gun sight. You've got to appreciate the logic of the naming. Those interested in the camping facilities here will find a total of 37 sites for tents and small RVs. Trail maps can be found at the guard station. If you happen here on one of the busy days, you can go to **Grande Ronde Lake,** which is just

In Granite, many of the old buildings still stand and some are in use.

a mile down the road from Anthony Lake. It is equally beautiful though smaller and its facilities are much more rustic.

Roughly 3 miles down the road, you'll come to Elkhorn Mountain Summit. At 7,392 feet high, this is the highest point on the Elkhorn Scenic Byway. For the next 20 miles or so, you will travel more of this serene winding road amid its calming scenery. The **Chinese Rock Walls** or **Ah Hee Diggings** are halfway between mileposts 45 and 46. They appear to be just large rocks moved by the elements, but when you get closer it's obvious that someone had moved them with a purpose. Once the more easily accessed gold was mined from the area, the mines were leased out to Asian immigrants. They reworked these same mines with efficiency and a small bit of success. As they wound their way down the river, they moved its rocks and boulders, in their search beneath the ground for gold. There are roughly 60 acres of the walls that can measure up to 15 feet wide and 12 feet high.

Once you come to the junction with FR 73, turn left (south) toward **Granite.** This will be your first place to stop for gas since leaving I-84. Although it is not really a "ghost town," Granite's boom was some time ago. The town's history started as many did in the West, with the discovery of gold. In this instance, it was found at Bull Run Creek in 1862. Over the next several decades, nearly 9 million dollars' worth of gold was mined in the area. In its heyday, Granite grew to a population of 5,000, which explains the abandoned buildings, both residential and business: This little town you see now once boasted a drugstore, two hotels (one with 50 rooms), a livery stable, a post office, five saloons, and three stores. Now the population is 24 at last count, making it the second-smallest incorporated city in Oregon. The town has an "I live here to be left alone" quality to it at first, but once you talk with a resident or two, you'll find they're quite cheerful and friendly.

As part of the Federal Writer's Project of the Great Depression, Mrs. Neil Niven, one of the town's first schoolteachers, was interviewed about her early life in Granite. Her interview gives you some idea of how rough and ready the West's mining towns were: "The men of Granite had a code of ethics that fulfilled the function of legal law. Oh, there were plenty of infractions of the code, but often these infractions were dealt with by lead logic, rather than by legal evasion. I suppose it isn't right to stretch a horse thief with his boots on, or lead up a sift snitcher, but it served its purpose with remarkable finality to further trespassing." She was also one of only four single women in town back then, so her dance card was never empty.

It's estimated that there were nearly 3,000 Chinese immigrants living in the Granite area during the good times. Back then, three stores in town were owned by Chinese-American merchants even while other local businesses, such as the town's Hotel Grand, advertised, "No Chinese Employed."

The Outback Gas Station and Café at the entrance to Granite (the only road into town) will be the first stop for gas since you left I-84. Folks in Granite would know best where to find fall's mushrooms and late summer's huckleberries along the byway. Be especially sure you know which mushrooms should be eaten and those that shouldn't. Since huckleberries (a relative of blueberries) have not been successfully commercially cultivated, the only way they get into jams, syrups, and other tasty treats is by picking them where they grow wild. They are best picked from mid-August to mid-September, when they're plump and a deep purple. If you happen upon a good patch, take what you want but not more than you need. Once picked, huckleberries have a very short shelf life. Pick some for yourself; leave the rest for other pickers and the local wildlife.

The original bank safe in Sumpter.

Once you leave Granite, you're more than halfway through this trip. Soon you'll see signs for **Blue Spring Summit,** a pretty busy and loud spot come winter. That's when snowmobile enthusiasts descend upon the 5,864-foot summit to enjoy 150 miles of groomed trails.

Just 15 miles from Granite is another not-quite "ghost town" born from mining madness, **Sumpter.** Originally called Fort Sumter (misspelled by the original founders), the name had to be changed because the 1883 postal service didn't accept the name. So "Fort" was dropped and the missing *t* was added. The real boom started after the Sumpter Valley Railroad reached town in 1896. By 1901, Sumpter had grown to more than 30,000 people and 81 business establishments. Two years later, the town had a brickyard, a sawmill, a smelter, electric lights, a fine gravity-flow water system with reservoir (still in use to this day), baseball and basketball teams, a racetrack, an undertaker, several assayers, a brewery, a dairy, two cigar factories, an extensive Chinatown, a hospital, more than a dozen saloons, livery stables, and blacksmith shops—also five hotels, a clothing store, three general stores, a public school with 200 students, an opera house, two banks, four churches, a telephone system, newspapers, and a fire department. Yet as early as 1905, the mines began to be depleted—and the town's residents fled.

To further the dissolving of Sumpter, in 1917 a hotel kitchen fire decimated almost every business and many homes in just three hours. The town's water supply failed after the first 30 minutes and dynamite had to be used to quell the flames. Only one building remained standing, the Hospital on the Hill, which later was used as a home, then abandoned and left to rot. Thankfully, it's recently been restored as a bed & breakfast.

Maybe the history of mining in America has never struck you as fascinating. Like most of the history we're taught in school, it's not riveting until experienced in person. Sumpter is so proud of its history that you can't help but walk away with at least some excitement about mining and its place in America's past. The **Sumpter Valley Dredge,** located within the 80-acre Oregon State Heritage Area has become a treasure trove of information about above-ground mining, though more gold was found in the area via underground mining. Besides explaining what a dredge is and how it works, the volunteers in the gift shop are very forthcoming with information about both mining and the area. Even if this doesn't seem like something you'd be interested in, take a few minutes to drive over and check it out. You'll see those minutes turn into an hour quickly. An information video is worth watching for background info on the area and the dredge itself. There are several well-groomed walking trails surrounding the dredge, each no more than a mile long. Rangers teach gold pan mining for free in the summer months. There's small fee only if you find any gold. Once your panning skills are mastered, the Powder River is just steps away. If that isn't enough, you can always hope to see the ghost of Chris Rowe, who succumbed as the only work-related death on the dredge. Looking for more historical mining widgets? Located at the east end of town in the **Cracker Creek Museum of Mining.** At this time, it's a self-guided tour of

The Sumpter Valley Dredge is even more interesting inside.

mining machines and tools. Work is being done to provide signage explaining how the items were used, and to build a structure to house the smaller artifacts. Until the latter is completed, the museum consists of a group of interesting industrial objects to inspect out in the clean mountain air.

The **Sumpter Community Flea Markets** held each Memorial, Independence, and Labor Day weekend are big events here. They started in the '70s as part of Sumpter Valley Days but were so popular that they grew into their own event. Vendors at the flea market can be found at the fairgrounds and museum, and in front of private residences. Beyond the myriad opportunities to browse and buy, you'll find live entertainment, food vendors, and a real feeling of community. These are busy weekends for any tourist town but when there are only 191 residents, everyone pitches in.

The aforementioned Mrs. Neil Niven of Granite was born in Sumpter. As a young woman, she won the title of Mill Queen, to dedicate the new mill. According to her, she was to pull on a cord connected to a whistle that was to announce the mill's opening. Just as she did so, the mill's foundation gave way and the building collapsed. It was never rebuilt.

The astonishing Elkhorn Mountains can be viewed at milepost 33. These mountains were created by three different natural events, during different eras. First, ancient seas deposited sedimentary rock, which was then bombarded by molten rock that became granite, followed by volcanic basalt; finally, the glaciers came ripping their way through the area, leaving behind the mountains and lakes.

If your travel plans have brought you to this area on a weekend between Memorial Day weekend and the end of September, schedule enough time to ride the **Sumpter Valley Railroad at McEwen Station.** For 30 years, volunteers have lovingly restored and run this narrow-gauge railway originally used from 1890 to 1964. The steam engine makes a 5-mile trek. The views and quaintness of the ride are hard to duplicate, further solidifying just how historically valuable this area is. For extra drama and excitement, "train robberies" are scheduled to occur at various times throughout the season. Depending on weather, Fall Foliage and Christmas rides may be available.

As you drive along, you'll see some things that resemble short telephone poles. **Mowich Loop Wildlife Viewing Area** is a picnic site with artificial snags (the big nests on posts) that, since they were erected in 1977, have been home to osprey and the occasional American bald eagle. Depending on the time of year, there's also a chance of seeing mule and white-tailed deer, and elk.

These man-made nests have been home to osprey and American bald eagles.

Because everywhere you turn here, mining's past influence is prevalent, you will also easily view the tailings left behind by the mining dredges, including the dredge you just toured. (If you're having difficulty spotting the tailings, vegetation has taken over: look for straight lines as if the plants were hoed.)

Just a couple of miles farther is **Union Creek Campground** and **Phillips Lake Reservoir.** This spot has something for just about everyone. There are 58 camping and RV sites—12 of which are tent only, 80 picnic areas, a fish-cleaning station, a boat ramp, and hiking trails. Along with being the biggest in the Wallowa-Whitman, this campground has that rarest of commodities in forest campgrounds—flush toilets. For those not stopping for the day or overnight but just for a bit, go a few miles down OR 7 to the **Powder River Interpretive Site.** Here you'll find a ½-mile paved, accessible trail and a fully accessible fishing platform. Being below the Mason Dam, the resident and hatchery trout fishing here is excellent.

As the drive winds down and scenery turns to small amiable farms, Baker City, the "Queen City of the Mines," arises and marks the end spot for this journey. But just because the mountains and lakes are behind you doesn't mean the trip is over. This town offers so much to visitors by wearing its historical heart on its sleeve. One hundred and ten buildings in Baker City on the National Register of Historic Places and it is the largest commercial historic district in Oregon. So park the car as soon as you get to Main Street to explore the very walkable downtown. Or take a ride on the **Baker City Trolley.** A round trip will take about an hour and is a nice way to look around without any worry of getting lost. During the warmer months, a horse-drawn carriage is also available: ask inside one of the hotels or restaurants for them to call the driver. Maps of walking tours through the Historic District are available at shops and hotels. The Natatorium (circa 1920) is a stone's throw from the town's glorious historic district and contains the **Baker Heritage Museum,** which houses an extensive collection of fossils and rocks, along with information and relics on the area's logging, ranching, farming, and of course mining.

The Queen City must have her castle. And so, the **Geiser Grand Hotel** has been faithfully and lovingly restored. Originally built in 1889, the property was 30 days from being demolished when Barbara and Dwight Sidway stepped in—to the relief of many local residents—and proceeded to save it, restore its elegance and bring it up to modern standards while retaining its charm. The project started in 1993 and took five years and 7

The official Elkhorn Scenic Byway includes OR 30 and the town of Haines, founded in 1885. A small town, frozen in time, known as the "Biggest Little City in Oregon," Haines has a museum packed with over 10,000 items. Sometimes called "Grandma's Attic," the **Eastern Oregon Museum** is located in an old high school gym. Once you're inside, it's easy to see how it can claim so many thousands of artifacts. Here's just a sampling: the bar from the no-longer-existing mining town of Bourne, a plethora of cowboy memorabilia, the entire Haines Railroad Depot, multiple carriages and surreys—some with fringe on top, 19th-century wedding dresses, more than 100 dolls, and a complete one-room schoolhouse with everything from inkwells to the working school bell. Once you've seen everything from Baker County, it's time to enjoy dinner with the locals. The **Haines Steak House** has an Old West look on the outside and resembles a busily decorated log cabin inside, augmented by items on loan from the museum. Nearby is the Chandler Cabin. Built in 1861, it's the first cabin in Baker County and was moved here in the 1990s. Be sure to look up at the hand-stenciled street signs.

million dollars to complete. Years of being ignored and abused had taken a steep toll on the building, from the basement's sitting in water to the catastrophic erosion caused by decades of nesting pigeons. It may be hard to believe how bad things were when you're standing under crystal chandeliers and amid stunning woodwork.

The hotel's welcoming bar is small but well lit and replete with a look of the establishment's original era without being kitschy. Barbara has an extensive background in historic restoration and strives to keep your overall experience genuine. Just past the front desk and open to the lobby is the restaurant. Above the tables is a resplendent stained-glass ceiling so well done, you'd swear that natural light were streaming in. If the history of the hotel interests you, be sure to head down to the basement to see all the items, photos, and historical documents pertaining to the hotel. There are some in the bar and lobby as well. On many Saturdays, a local docent dresses in period-style costume and gives a tour of the premises, filling you in on the lore of the Geiser Grand: the bullet holes in the lion's head, the original use for the library, and how the now-extinct underground tunnel system in town fed into the hotel.

The Geiser family originally built the hotel to be the finest between

Seattle and Salt Lake City. Theirs was only the third elevator building west of the Mississippi. The hotel also had electricity and ice cream brought in by train. But the guest rooms back then were smaller and some lacked a private bathroom. Today, the accommodations range from three types of suites to two types of rooms. All are decorated in classical and demure fabrics and colors that evoke the hotel's original style. Every suite has 10-foot-tall windows and some have views of the nearby mountains. All of the rooms have 14-foot ceilings, crystal chandeliers, plush robes, and complimentary WiFi. The staff from check-in to checkout show pride in their hotel while exuding a warmth that is rarely found at fine hotels in bigger cities.

It doesn't get much grander than the Geiser Grand Hotel in Baker City.

It's amazing how much there is to see or do in a town of 10,000. Main Street between Auburn to the south and Campbell to the north is well laid out for shopping and sightseeing. If the sun is shining too brightly, one side of the street is often in the shade. And unlike in some towns with tourist-friendly shopping, you'll be surrounded by folks who actually live there and who believe wholeheartedly in "shopping local." Main Street is the area's primary shopping district and of the 166 businesses in Baker City, 142 are local.

The cowboy way is still alive and well in eastern Oregon, and **Boots Leonard Gallery and Studio** has what every mountain man and woman needs: buckskin. Here you can purchase handcrafted buckskin clothing and accessories. If you're

Honest-to-goodness craftsmanship at the Boots Leonard Gallery.

lucky, you'll find Ronald Dempsey making one of his practically indestructible but oh-so-soft pieces. Looking like a Daniel Boone or Grizzly Adams, Ronald stands out. His jackets, hats, and accessories are beautiful to behold and he takes custom orders as well. The gallery features western clothing and art but isn't stuffy nor kitschy. As you stroll along, there are plenty of spots to stop for a nosh, drink, or meal. And thankfully, nothing feels as if it's just here for tourists. Visit **Charlie's Ice Cream Parlor** for a cool treat. Sweets lovers should make a beeline for **The Sycamore Tree,** to relish a multitude of fudges, from those with traditional flavors to others with a slight twist. Some flavors may not sound good at first, such as orange cream, root beer float, or pumpkin pie, but doubters will be believers after a generous free sample. The store also carries Fiesta Ware, work by local artists, and many country and Victorian gift items. **Marilyn's Music** carries many items musicians want or need, whether they be expert or novice. Just follow the loud music emanating from the speakers at the front door. Nearby is what may be the largest bookstore in eastern Oregon, **Betty's Books.** Those interested in learning more about Oregon history will find a very nice selection here. Healthy and simple living applies to everything at **Bella Main Street Market,** from the groceries and wine, to the décor items and coffee bar. And to go along with your organic fair trade coffee, be sure to try one of the zucchini muffins. They're made for the shop by a local baker and they are divine. The proprietor makes local deliveries on her bike. As Baker City is a very bike-friendly place, Bella also carries the legendary Baker City bike jersey. The shirt's fun silk-screened art is from a local artist and makes great souvenir.

Returning to the Geiser Grand Hotel, you can dine at the **Geiser Grill.**

The dining room sits directly below the lovely stained-glass ceiling, but this being eastern Oregon, fancy dress is not required. Menu items include steaks cut in-house, trout from nearby Idaho, and surprisingly tasty coconut shrimp. All ingredients are fresh, and local whenever possible. Be sure to save room for bread pudding with whiskey sauce. On Wednesday nights there's an all-you-can-eat pasta bar set up in a separate room. You choose what you'd like in your dish (German sausage, seafood, and plenty more choices) and it's cooked right there before your eyes. It's fresh and a great bargain. Across from the hotel is **Mad Matilda's,** a large and airy coffeehouse that serves freshly made soup, scones, light breakfast and lunch items, and gelato made not too far away in Boise. There is also an Internet-connected computer for customers. Family vacations should include at least one eat-in-your-car burger; make this one from **Burger Bob's.** Messy, huge burgers and thick, real milkshakes—what more do you need?

IN THE AREA

Accommodations

Anthony Lake Guard Station and Campground, Anthony Lake. 37 tent sites, 10 for RV. Open May through Nov. Call 541-523-4476.

Always Welcome Inn, 175 Campbell Street, Baker City. Call 541-523-3431. A good bargain with a really nice view. A fossil bed for excavating behind the hotel makes this one-of-a-kind lodging. Web site: www.alwayswelcomeinn.com.

Depot Inn, 179 South Mill Street, Sumpter. Call 541-894-2522. All 14 rooms are nonsmoking. Web site: www.thedepotinn-sumpter.com.

Lazy Moose Cabin, three blocks east of downtown Sumpter. Call 541-894-2414. A modern one-room cabin with RV hookups, too.

McCulley Fork Campground, about 12 miles southeast of Granite on FR 73. This small first-come, first-served spot has a specially designated site for recreational gold panning.

Oregon Trail Motel, 211 Bridge Street, Baker City. Call 541-523-5844. River-view rooms available. Pet friendly.

Sumpter Bed & Breakfast, 344 NE Columbia Street, Sumpter. Call 541-894-0048 or 1-800-287-5234. The only building in the town's business district left after the devastating 1917 fire was the Hospital on the Hill. It's now a B&B whose menu includes huckleberry pancakes. Web site: www.sumpterbb.com.

Sumpter Pines RV Park, 640 South Sumpter Highway, 1 mile east of Sumpter. Call 541-894-2328. This Good Sam park is open year-round, welcomes dogs, and has 17 spaces with full hookups and four tent spaces.

Sumpter Stockade, 129 East Austin, Sumpter. Call 541-894-2360. Besides offering rooms, allows campers to pay to pitch a tent in the private yard. Open mid-Apr. through mid-Oct.

Union Creek Campground, 20 miles west of Baker City on OR 7. Call 541-523-4476. Open mid-May to late Nov. Web site: www.publiclands .org.

Attractions and Recreation

Anthony Lakes Ski Resort. The highest base elevation in Oregon may have been hard on pioneers, but it's great for skiers who will find both Nordic and downhill here. Web site: www.anthonylakes.com.

Baker City Trolley, eight stops citywide, Baker City. Call 541-523-6561. Main Street stop at Washington. Arrives in each direction once an hour; check posted schedule. Web site: www.neotransit.org.

Baker Heritage Museum, 2480 Grove Street, Baker City. Call 541-523-9308. Web site: www.bakerheritagemusuem.com.

Bella Main Street Market, 2023 Main Street, Baker City. Call 541-523-7490. Organic coffee, groceries, wine, and astounding breakfast muffins. Web site: www.bellabakercity.com.

Celtic Festival, Fairgrounds, 2610 Grove Street, Baker City. Festival plus highland games, entertainment, and sheep dog trials. Some events can be entered the same day. Web site: www.bakerhighlanders.org.

Community Flea Market, Sumpter. Call 541-894-2314. Each Memorial, Independence, and Labor Day weekend, eastern Oregon's largest flea market takes over Sumpter. Web site: www.sumpter.org.

Cracker Creek Museum, 2465 18th Street, Sumpter. Call 541-523-3381. Self-guided outdoor tours of historically significant underground mining equipment from the area

The Drudge Shop, Cemetery Road, Sumpter. Call 541-894-2203. Mining supplies and detectors.

Eastern Oregon Museum, 14514 Muddy Creek Lane, Haines. Call 541-856-3233. 10,000 artifacts in an old high school gym. Closed Mon. and Tues. Web site: www.hainesoregon.com.

Elkhorn Classic, Baker City and surrounding areas. A three-day, four-stage race held each June. www.elkhornclassic.com

Fall Festival, Baker City. Call 541-523-5442. Each September for one Saturday. Includes a Dutch oven cook-off, pie-eating contest, cowboy poetry, and hayrides.

Geiser Grand Hotel Tour, 1996 Main Street, Baker City. Call 541-523-1889 or 1-888-434-7374. Costumed docents lead tours of the historic hotel. Every Sat. at 3:30 PM. Reservations suggested. Web site: www.geisergrand.com.

Historic Homes Tour, Baker City. See inside some of the valley's oldest homes during a five-hour tour. Call 541-523-5442.

Marilyn's Music, 1821 Main Street, Baker City. Call 541-523-3848. A locally owned music store. Web site: www.nwmusicplus.com.

Miner's Jubilee, Geiser-Pollman Park and Fairgrounds, 2610 Grove Street, Baker City. Call 541-523-5606. Each July, this traditional event includes a quilt show, parade, and bronc and bull riding.

The Outback at Granite, Granite (town entrance). Call 541-755-5300. Diner, bar, groceries, souvenirs.

Powder River Threadworks, 1705 Main Street, Baker City. Call 541-523-4272. Vintage quilts, fabrics, and linens.

The Sumpter Dredge. Call 541-894-2472. Tour inside and out of the last of three gold dredges used in Sumpter back in the days when corporate gold mining was king of the town. Web site: www.friendsofthedredge .com.

Sumpter Valley Railroad, Oregon Highway 7, 7 miles east of Sumpter. Call 541-894-2268. Ride in original railroad cars pulled by original steam locomotives. Web site: www.svry.com.

The Sycamore Tree, 2108 Main Street, Baker City. Call 541-523-4840. A home décor and gift store with outstanding homemade fudge. Web site: www.sycamoregifts.com.

T&T Wildlife Tours, 8 miles west off exit 285 (I-84) on North Powder River Lane. Follow "Wildlife Viewing" signs. Call 541-856-3356. Take the only horse-drawn Rocky Mountain elk viewing tour. The tour is narrated and inexpensive. Weekends only, Dec. through Feb. Web site: www.tnt horsemanship.com.

U.S. Bank Gold Display, 2000 Main Street, Baker City. The gold nugget collection, including the Armstrong nugget weighing 80.4 ounces, can be viewed during normal banking hours. Web site: www.sumpteroregon gold.org.

Dining

Baker Bistro, 1925 Washington Avenue, Baker City. Call 541-523-9797. Breakfast and lunch.

Burger Bob's Drive-In, 2380 10th Street, Baker City. Call 541-523-3513. No tables, just a bench to eat on if you don't eat in your car. Famous for the ¾-pound Monster Double Decker burger, a half-gallon milkshake, and a spicy Screaming Weenie.

Charlie's Ice Cream Parlor, 2101 Main Street, Baker City. Call 541-524-9307. Soup and salads, too.

Coffee Corral, 1706 Campbell Street, Baker City. Call 541-524-9290. Conveniently located across the street from the Baker Heritage Museum. Bean roasting done on premises.

Haines Steak House, 910 Front Street, Haines. Call 541-856-3639. Local beef in a rustic setting. Closed Tues. Web site: www.hainessteakhouse .com.

Inland Café, 2715 10th Street, Baker City. Call 541-523-9041. Where the locals get home-cooked food.

Mad Matilda's, 1917 Main Street, Baker City. Call 541 523 4588.

Paizano's Pizza, 2940 10th Street, Baker City. Call 541-524-1000. Fresh and delicious salads along with stromboli. Gluten-free pizza crust available. Web site: www.PaizanosPizza.com

Scoop N Steamer Station, 363 Mill Street, Sumpter. Breakfast, lunch, dinner, ice cream, and espresso. Open year-round. Call 541-894-2236.

Other Contacts

Base Camp Baker. Trip planning and information. Call 1-800-523-1235. Web site: www.basecampbaker.com.

Baker Ranger District. Call 541-523-4476.

Baker County Visitors Center, 490 Campbell Street, Baker City. Call 541-523-5855. Web site: www.visitbaker.com.

Eastern Oregon Visitors Association. Call 1-800-332-1843. Web site: www.eova.com.

Wallowa County Chamber of Commerce, 115 Tejaka Lane, Enterprise. Call 541-426-4622. Web site: www.wallowacountychamber.com.

CHAPTER

9

To Hells Canyon with You

The Northeast Corner

Estimated length: 215 miles
Estimated time: 6 to 8 hours, but best with an overnight stay

Getting There: This is another great trip for those driving though Oregon with a final destination in mind but some spare time for exploring. Although it centers on Hells Canyon, the drive also skirts the south end of Eagle Cap Wilderness. The surrounding area that includes Eagle Cap and Wallowa Lake has been called "America's Little Switzerland" or the "Alps of America." The trip can be taken as this chapter is laid out, from the south end at OR 86 to FR 39, which becomes OR 82 and heads northwest to La Grande and back to I-84. Or, from La Grande, you can follow the above directions backward. Either way, you end up back on the interstate 45 miles from where you got off. Be sure to carry extra water. In winter, FR 39 is closed.

Highlights: If all high school students took a field trip to **Hells Canyon,** their geology class would be a breeze. The canyon is a textbook example of what happened when nature's different materials interacted during different stages of the earth's development, in this case to make our country's deepest gorge. Hells Canyon beats the Grand Canyon by quite a bit. Thanks

A salvaged cabin at Gangloff Park in La Grande.

to the diverse landscape, there are so many outdoor recreational activities here, the area could use a cruise director: hiking, fishing, hunting, camping, biking, wildlife viewing, spectacular photo opportunities, and much more.

This trip starts where the last one left off, at **Baker City,** which is strategically located for those who wish to take their time to get to know eastern Oregon: Hells Canyon to the east, the Elkhorn Mountains to the west, and other points of interest directly off I-84. The area has shopping, dining, historic homes and lodging, events, and neighborly residents. As this book was being written, work was being done on Blue Mountain Heritage Trail, set to open in 2010. This will be an 870-mile-loop trail similar to those found in Great Britain, linking historic sites, small Main streets, rivers, and much more. You can read more about Baker City in the previous chapter. But if you have any questions, just ask a resident. They're only too proud to show off their town.

Leaving from Baker City or I-84, you'll be taking OR 86 east. About 5 miles later, on the right, is the turnoff for **The National Historic Oregon Trail Interpretive Center**. This isn't just a room of dusty stuff or family treasures; it is a modern, well-thought-out building that does a very good job of teaching folks what it took, from beginning to end, to get across the Oregon Trail. If you were an elementary student in the mid-'80s to mid-'90s, the center will teach so much more than the Oregon Trail video game ever did. The first section of the self-guided tour is a little heavy handed. But for those not into reading every sign posted at historical landmarks, this display makes it clear just how difficult it was on the trail and how varied the pioneers were. After this, it's gets much better. There's a puzzle to see how to pack your wagon, as well as explanations on everything from the stoves designed just for the trail (and that proved completely useless) to how folks celebrated the few good times. The exhibits can be methodically or briefly visited, depending on your interest. All of the above makes this a great spot for kids and adults.

The highlight of the Oregon Trail Interpretive Center, though, may be that you can hike down (about ¾ mile each way) to get a close look at ruts left in the dirt by the many wagons coming through on the trail. A total of 4.2 miles of barrier-free trail loops around the center. On the trail are historic sites, viewpoints, shade structures, and benches. There are no restrooms, however, and you will need to bring your own water. Often, depending on the time of year there are interesting and informative events

Locals and visitors receive a hearty welcome at Annie's Café in Richland.

here. These range from stargazing and video presentations to live per-formances and cooking lectures, all related to the Oregon Trail.

On your left, between mile posts 30 and 31, is a display sign explain-ing the Hole-in-the-Wall landslide. In 1984, a lot of rain fell here for sev-eral days. All that seeping water, and perhaps a few tremors, brought millions of tons of earth that had been there for millennia down to the road you're now driving on. You can actually see the line in the earth showing where the ground used to be.

The first town you'll come to is **Richland,** a sweet little spot with the Hitching Post, a general store, and a charming diner called Annie's Café. Hopefully there'll be a special of waffles and fresh berries the day you visit. It's worth ordering even if you're there for lunch. With a population of about 250, that's about all you'll find in town. But, the first stop you should make in Richland, even if it's your only one, is **Eagle Creek Orchard.** If you arrive at the right time of year, you'll find tongue-tingling juicy peach-es. Seventeen different varieties are grown here. If the day is very warm and the bees would like the fruit, too, it's moved into a walk-in cooler, mak-ing the peaches delightfully cold on a hot summer day. The orchard is certified organic, watered by Eagle Creek, and all the fruit is tree ripened and handpicked. These aren't just terms used for marketing, it's the growers' philosophy. Owners Robert and Linda Cordtz also grow nectarines, plums, apricots, apples (nine varieties), pears (nine varieties), walnuts, and hazelnuts. You can miss the sign if you're not careful. Once you enter Richland, the road splits; be sure to veer to the left (toward New Bridge). This is a very family-friendly area, be sure to watch your speed, as kids may be returning home from school or playing with chums. Don't be surprised if a Becky Thatcher–like big sister and her little brother smile and wave as you drive by. On your left, that's Mill Pond. As you get to New Bridge, take a left. Take another left on Old Foothill Road. Black and yellow signs show the way.

Just as you leave town, **Farewell Bend State Recreation Area** at **Brownlee Reservoir** offers tent camping, a boat launch, horseshoe pits, and a sand volleyball court. Along with RV dump stations and tent camping sites, there are two rustic log cabins that can sleep up to four. From Memorial Day through Labor Day, many interpretive programs are scheduled. This was the last resting spot before the Oregon Trail pioneers turned off the Snake River after following it for 330 miles. If you explore north of the park, you may come upon ruts made by their wagon wheels.

What is it about the town of **Halfway?** The moment you enter it, you'll be conniving to stay here longer. It's so welcoming and tranquil at the same time, like the alluring towns in *Twilight Zone* episodes where the main character knows he should return to his own era but doesn't care to. "Midway" was the name the original residents wrote on their application to the U.S. Post Office. The answer that came back was that there already was a Midway in Oregon (where, this author knows not) and the name Halfway was suggested. During the now infamous dot.com explosion, the town was renamed halfway.com, becoming the nation's first locale to identify itself as an Internet address. Someday this will be in history books showing the technological boom's effects, like that of television's golden age on Truth or Consequences, New Mexico.

As you enter town, take Main Street straight through until you come to the local neighborhoods. This way you can make your way through town as you head back to OR 86. You can also park and walk the entire amiable downtown. The first stop is **Lillies of the Valley.** Depending on the time of day, teas and sometimes breakfast are served here. Just sitting among the many blooms in its garden would convert even the staunchest tea dis-

The garden at Lillies of the Valley.

liker. The building originally served as a doctor's home and practice. Owner Denise has converted it to a comfortable shabby-chic collection of sitting rooms designed for lounging with your tarts and tea. The formal teas are available by reservation. You can choose from a smaller Garden Tea or a more substantial Queen's Tea. If you happen to arrive on a Friday or Saturday, breakfast does not need a reservation and may include homemade cinnamon rolls, French toast with fresh local berries, weather permitting, may be served in a petite garden. After tea or breakfast, head back down Main Street from the direction you came, for some shopping. **Halfway Whimsical** carries Oregon artists from the very area you're traveling through. The focus in this volunteer-staffed store is on items made with reclaimed or recycled materials. You'll also find antiques, clothing, jewelry, wood crafts, and hand-stitched dolls. **Bri & TJ's Place** carries cigars, liquor, flasks, and gift items for motorcycle lovers and those who love them. And it just wouldn't be a visit to Halfway without a stop at **Quilts Plus,** a country store with antiques, fabric, and espresso drinks.

While visiting this neck of Oregon, stopping by a ghost town is almost required. **Cornucopia** is only 11 miles north of Halfway on the well-maintained gravel Halfway/Cornucopia Road. At one time, half of all Oregon's gold came out of these mines. Between 1880 and 1903, the market value on the 270,000 ounces excavated here valued over a million dollars. At today's values, that's over 100 million dollars. Then on Halloween of 1941, the mines closed unexpectedly. This was partly due to production's decline and World War II. In 24 hours, most of the 700 residents had left. The road up to Cornucopia was called "bootlegger grade," as it was built by county prisoners during the Prohibition days. At one time Cornucopia was the largest gold ghost town in Oregon, but weather does take its toll. Although they are dilapidated due to time and harsh winters, many of the buildings still stand and some equipment was left behind. On the other side of Pine Creek is **Cornucopia Lodge.** There are some really great photo opportunities here. The road is closed during the winter.

Go back to OR 86 and head east until FR 39, then turn left (north). You've now entered the very southern tip of **Hells Canyon National Recreation Area.** Classified as a wilderness in 1975, the area is comprised of just less than 215,000 acres. The canyon itself is 10 miles wide and the deepest gorge in North America. The Snake River is responsible for the razor-sharp geologic cuts that created this canyon. Before it was dammed up, the river was fast, hard, and powerful. Not that it isn't still a river to be reckoned with; just that it was much more so before the Brownlee, Oxbow, and Hells Canyon dams were put in place.

While you're enjoying the scenery, keep an eye out for cattle wandering out onto the road. This area has been used for horse and cattle grazing for centuries, starting with the Nez Perce Indians. Later settlers grazed sheep, cattle, and horses. The number of grazing animals is significantly less than it once was, but it's a good idea to stay alert as you come around the bend.

Explorers, trappers, pioneers, and anyone else coming upon Hells Canyon in the old days had only to glance into the chasms and at the lava rock walls, to decide to take long detours. Robert Stewart, an explorer, described it as "mountains appear here as if piled upon mountains." Some Oregon Trail folks thought that continuing to follow the Snake River might be the shortcut that so many were seeking. Only a lucky few returned to the Oregon Trail. Both access roads and trails begin to open in June, remaining open until September or October.

At milepost 29 on FR 39 is the turnoff to **Hells Canyon Overlook** on FR 3965, a 3-mile detour off the main route. The view is quite panoramic but may be disappointing to those looking for the tumultuous Snake River. For that you'd need to travel to Hat Point Lookout, which is many miles of rough road from here. This vantage point is behind Hells Canyon Dam and therefore only the tamed Snake River may be seen, if it can be spotted at all from here. The canyon you're looking at is McGraw Creek. It's still well worth the detour to Hells Canyon Overlook.

Farther down FR 39 (about 12 miles) you'll find **Salt Creek Summit,** a snow park for winter sports enthusiasts, especially snowmobilers but also snowshoers and backcountry skiers. It's also a trailhead for the beloved Eagle Cap Wilderness to the west and Wallowa Valley Ranger District to the east. Next to the Salt Creek Summit Multi-Purpose Building, you'll find rustic toilets and an information kiosk on the aforementioned winter activities. The Tenderfoot Wagon Road is also here (check the kiosk for location), built in 1903 as the road to the Tenderfoot Mine. The logs laid to mark the original road can still be seen. This trail is also popular with mountain bikers.

Leaving FR 39, head west on OR 82. **Joseph** might be described as the artist's heart of this rugged region. This is by far the most tourist-oriented town in the Hells Canyon region. Still, except during the peak of the season, it's not nearly as crowded as other vacation spots. Lots of shopping, dining, and sightseeing are available in Joseph. **Calderas of Joseph** is one those benefits of this being an artsy town. The bistro-style fare features local veggies and a daily special fondue. Next door, you'll find the exact opposite at **R&R Drive-In,** where locals eat. If you're ready for real food without fancy art on the walls, this is the place for you. While eating, you'll see everyone from cowhands to forest firefighters come in. Although the Main

A burner left from Halfway's sawmill days.

Street here is wider than those of the towns you've just come through, it's easily navigable. The Art Walk takes you past seven bronze sculptures, all made by one of the three local foundries, one of which is Valley Bronze. Now the premier fine-art foundry in the Pacific Northwest, when it opened in 1982 it was the first one in Joseph. Recently Valley Bronze produced pieces that are part of the National World War II Memorial in Washington, D.C. They've also been asked by the National Archives to frame the Declaration of Independence. Foundry tours are offered but it's best to call ahead or check with their Main Street gallery.

The picturesque **Wallowa Lake** is just a mile south of Joseph. Geology buffs say it's a perfect example of a morainal, or ribbon, lake. That's because about 15,000 years ago (give or take a few thousand), a deep glacier cut and pressed a path. Once the climate warmed and the glacier receded, it left a 299-foot-deep lake that stretches for 5 miles. However it got here, once you come to see it, you'll be glad you did. Between the mountains, the lake, and the wildflowers, you may have an overwhelming urge to start singing about the hills being alive with the sound of music. It's near here that you will find the grave of Elder Chief Joseph of the Nez Perce tribe. It was his son, Young Chief Joseph, who refused to move his tribe to Idaho as mandated by the U.S. government. He and his tribe battled to stay in their land as promised to them by U.S. treaty. To briefly summarize the stories of the betrayal of the Nez Perce here would be to do them an injustice, and their story is already riddled with injustices. If the beauty of the land here moves you, make the effort to learn more about the story of the Nez Perce tribe, and Elder and Younger Chief Joseph.

"Wallowa" translates from the Nez Perce language as "winding water" or "fish trap," depending upon whom you ask. There's a legendary tale in which their chief's beloved daughter and her new husband—from a neighboring tribe they once feuded with—were paddling on the lake. Their union upset the Great Spirit and a giant serpent snatched them away while both tribes stood helpless, watching. Throughout the decades, sightings of a Loch Ness–like monster surfaced. The last time was in 1985. You'll most likely find trophy-class Kokanee and lake, brook, and bull trout in the lake these days.

At the south end of Wallowa Lake is one of the best ways to see its beauty and the surrounding prairies and mountains: the **Wallowa Lake Tramway.** After a 15-minute ride 3,700 feet up Mount Howard, you'll find food at Summit Grill, amazing views, and 2.5 miles of walking trails. The trails are easy, short, and have views that will astound. The tram was built in 1970 for a ski resort that never manifested. Luckily for us the tram stuck around.

Once you leave Joseph and continue on through Wallowa County, most everything here has to do with the great outdoors—fishing, hunting, hiking, climbing, and so forth. Even if you don't participate in these types of hobbies, you can still appreciate the land and all it offers. The first town you arrive at is **Enterprise,** just 6 miles down the road from

Joseph. Here you'll find the U.S. Forest Service–run **Wallowa Mountain Visitor Center** and terrifically informative maps, displays, and geological information. This is a great for planning extensive hiking or just day trips. Oregon is known throughout the world for its micro-brew beers. And whether you're a beer connoisseur or just like the taste of a tall, smooth lager, then a stop at **Terminal Gravity Brewery** is highly recommended. The IPA made here with spring water and Eagle Cap snow melt has been called one of the best beers in Oregon. The brewery is a Craftsman-style house so the predominant amount of seating is outdoors, and there's a full menu. For another dining experience, there's the **RimRock Inn and Restaurant.** The food is well executed and the service very hospitable. But what seals the deal is the stupendous view of Joseph Canyon. It's so jaw dropping that you have to remind yourself to close your mouth and chew. And if you're the type who doesn't mind trading in modern amenities for views of nature's graceful splendor, check ahead to see if one their tepees is available. They can be very popular so don't leave this one to the last minute; make reservations well in advance. Get to know the area with experts with **Wallowa Resources,** which provides naturalist-guided hikes in winter and summer. The hikes range in length for most ages and abilities, and are a half or full day. The winter hike is done on snowshoes. In the summer, you can choose from various hikes. The Buckhorn Overlook hike is a full-day hike that gets to those views of Hells Canyon and Snake River that are missed at Hells Canyon Overlook. The Birding and Wildflower hikes are a half day. There are more to choose from; what's available depends on the season.

Where there was once mining and/or logging, there were trains. In Wallowa, you can take the **Eagle Cap Excursion Train** and just sit back and enjoy the view. The tracks are owned by Wallowa and Union counties and operated by the Wallowa Union Railroad Authority. Many of the trips serve a meal and there's a concession stand on board, too. If you brought your pup along for the trip, call ahead about the local pet sitter. The most frequent trips—the Two Rivers and Spirit of Wallowa—depart at 10 AM. The more sporting rail rider might wish to try the River to Rail or Fish Train for something different. One involves riding the Wallowa River before boarding and the other, remote steelhead fishing holes. As the trains leave in the morning, it's most convenient to stay in Wallowa, and luckily the **Mingo Motel** is here. This quaint motor-motel is so well executed it could rightfully be called the nicest lodging in Wallowa. Which it is, and not just

True on-the-road comfort can be found at the Mingo Motel.

because it's the only lodging in Wallowa. Owners and managers, Chase and Dina Ence, have done a bang-up job of making their place comfortable, relaxing, and sweet. All the log cabin furniture in the rooms is made nearby from local wood. The décor is enchanting, with grizzly bear lamps and quilts to match. Even the mattress is comfortable, much more so than some better big-city hotels. There's cable and WiFi and locally aromatherapy soaps. It's so effortless to stay at the Mingo Motel. Just pull in, check in, and walk mere steps to your room. Across the highway and a block east is **Blonde Strawberry,** so getting a latte and scone will be easy, too.

Named after a popular song in the day about a ship lost on Lake Michigan, Elgin is a sleepy little town. But if you get here during their big events—Riverfest or the Stampede Rodeo—this little town is certainly awakened. The interesting **Elgin Opera House** was built in 1912 to distract from a nearby house of ill repute and is still in use as a single-screen movie theater and stage for local music and theater productions. Its slanted seating and superb acoustics were pretty high-tech for its time. And because it put Elgin's city hall and theater in the same building, it's considered very unusual, maybe the only one of its kind. In recent years, the building has been renovated and placed on the National Register of Historic Buildings. Three miles north of town is the Rockwall Escarpment and ice caves, a unique spot for exploring and rock climbing. Although it's been used for climbing since the '70s, there aren't many climbers in the area and therefore it is not busy.

It may not look like it now, but **Island City** was originally an island (roughly 8 miles long and ¾ miles across) situated between a slough and La Grande River. The slough was diverted and the island was no more. A fun diversion is **D&B Supply Company,** similar to the general stores once found in all small towns across America. This one has live chicks and bunnies, cowboy boots, and giant bags of animal feed. There's a nice selection of farm and ranch toys to take home to your favorite city kid.

Now you've come to the last destination on this trip: La Grande. But first a few words about pronunciation. Although the second part of the town's name may look like the word used to order a medium latte at a certain coffee chain, this is not how it is said. Just pretend the *e* isn't there and say it as almost one word: "Lagrand." La Grande is the largest town on this trip, with more than 12,000 residents. So far along your journey, you've seen trains and wagon train ruts. What's left? How about fire engines? The **Eastern Oregon Fire Museum** is housed in La Grande's historic fire station (circa 1899). Climbing on the vintage engines is allowed and even encouraged. It's a great spot to take kids and photos. Speaking of kids, if you're staying over in La Grande, see what's playing at **La Grande Drive-In.** Movies are shown throughout the summer, Thursday through Sunday. Wonder what one does with a historic financial building with 20-foot-high windows? If the building is in Oregon, there's a good chance it will turn into a micro-brewery. The **Mt. Emily Ale House** serves a full menu, including pizza. Minors are welcome for dining. If you've had enough cowboy art, there's **Satellite Gallery,** which supports local artists. And at **Potter's House,** raku pottery is displayed in a restored Queen Anne home.

Depending on which direction on I-84 you're heading after La Grande, there's still one more place to check out. On the north end of town where OR 30 meets I-84 is **Gangloff Park.** Here you'll find a log cabin that was created by using four old salvaged cabins. It has paved walking trails and a wide view of the Grande Ronde Valley. If you're still looking for Oregon's critters, then the **Ladd Marsh Wildlife Area** can be found south of town: take exit 268, head west and follow the signs. The 3,000-plus acres offer plenty of opportunities for bird-watching. You can walk the new nature trail or drive along the marsh on Peach Road.

IN THE AREA

Accommodations

Bronze Antler Bed & Breakfast, 309 South Main Street, Joseph. Call 541-432-0230 or 866-520-9769. Perfect for those wanting to stay right in the heart of Joseph. Web site: www.bronzeantler.com.

Clear Creek Inn, 48212 Clear Creek Road, Halfway. Call 541-742-2238. An 1891 farmhouse with breakfast and dinner service. Web site: www.clearcreekinn.com.

Cornucopia Lodge, 12 miles north of Halfway. Call 1-800-742-6115. Located in true wilderness. At 4,700 feet above sea level, it can take some adjusting. Web site: www.cornucopialodge.com

Farewell Bend State Recreation Area, Richland. Call 541-869-2365 or 1-800-551-6949 for information only, 1-800-452-5687 for reservations. Located on the west end of Brownlee Reservoir. Open year-round with 30 tent sites and two log cabins. Web site: www.oregonstateparks.org.

Hu-Na-Ha RV Park, 255 Cedar Street, Elgin. Call 541-437-2253. A newer RV park on La Grande River. Tent camping available, too, with restrooms and kitchenette counters. Web site: www.eoni.com/~elgin.

Hurricane Creek Campground, 6 miles south of Enterprise on Highway 82 and FR 8205.

Indian Lodge Motel, 201 South Main Street, Joseph. Call 541-432-2651 or 1-888-286-5484. Web site: www.eoni.com.

Matterhorn Swiss Village, 59950 Wallowa Lake Highway, Joseph. Call 541-432-4071. Web site: www.matterhornswissvillage.com.

Minam River Lodge, Minam. Call 541-432-6545. Getting to the lodge takes guided horseback provided by the lodge or hike. Web site: www.minamlodgeoutfitters.com.

Mingo Motel, 102 North Alder Street, Enterprise. Call 541-886-2021. A complete redo makes this classic motor motel a delightful stay.

Mountain View Motel RV Park, 83450 Joseph Highway, Joseph. Call 541-432-2982 or 1-866-262-9891.

Pine Valley Lodge, 163 North Main Street, Halfway. Call 541-742-2027. Web site: www.pvlodge.com.

Stampede Inn, 51 South Seventh Avenue, Elgin. Call 541-437-2441 or 1-877-769-7600. Classic motor motel with pet-friendly rooms. Web site: www.stampedeinn.com.

Wallowa Lake Lodge, 60060 Wallowa Lake Highway, Wallowa Lake. Call 541-432-9821. Built in 1923, then restored in 1928, it is open year-round. Originally part of an amusement park that was destroyed by heavy snows in 1940. Web site: www.wallowalake.com.

Attractions and Recreation

Bri & TJ's Place, Main Street, Halfway. Motorcycle for the hobbyist or lifer.

Chief Joseph Days Rodeo, Joseph. The last weekend in July. Web site: www.chiefjosephdays.com.

Cornucopia, 11 miles north of Halfway. A mining ghost town with buildings still, but barely, standing.

D&B Supply Co., 10101 East First Street, Island City. Call 541-963-8466. Web site: www.dbsupply.com.

Eagle Cap Excursion Train, 402 Fifth Street, Wallowa, or 300 North Eighth Street, Elgin. Call 1-800-848-9969. Excursions depart at 10 AM. The gift shop and concession stand take cash only. Web site: www.eagle captrain.com.

Eagle Cap Wilderness Pack Station, 59761 Wallowa Lake Highway, Joseph. Call 541-432-4145 or 1-800-681-6222. Guided horseback: one- to two-hour rides, half-day or all-day rides, overnight trips, three- or five-day guided trips. Web site: www.eaglecapwildernesspackstation.com.

Eagle Creek Orchard, 43479 Old Foothill Road, New Bridge (Richland). Call 541-893-6790. Fruit too good to pass up. Well worth the side trip.

Outside the National Historic Oregon Trail Interpretive Center.

Open daily, May through Oct. Web site: www.eaglecreekorchard.com.

Eastern Oregon Fire Museum, 102 Elm Street, La Grande. Call 541-963-8588. Five vintage and antique fire engines, plus equipment and informative displays.

Elgin Historical Museum, 104 North Eighth Street, Elgin. Call 541-437-2014.

Four Seasons Fly Shoppe, Highway 82, Island City. Call 541-963-8420. The largest full-service fly-fishing store in Eastern Oregon. Web site: www.4seasonsfly.com.

Halfway Whimsical, 231 Gover Lane, Halfway. Call 541-742-6040. Features eco-friendly art by local artists. Web site: www.halfwaywhimsical .com.

Hell's Canyon Adventures, Oxbow. Call 541-785-3352. All levels of whitewater adventures, including family friendly. Web site: www.hells canyonadventures.com.

Hells Canyon Motorcycle Rally, Hells Canyon. Second weekend in June. The large event brings the big crowds to the area and NO VACANCY signs from Baker City and along Hells Canyon Byway. Web site: www.hellscanyonrally.com.

Hells Canyon Mule Days, Enterprise. Three-day event held each September that includes a parade, a barbecue, horse and mule sales, and a quilt show.

Hurricane Llama Treks, near Enterprise. Call 541-928-2850 or 1-866-386-8735. Four guide-led llama trips are scheduled each summer. Web site: www.hdtrek.com.

La Grande Drive-In, 404 20th Street, La Grande. Call 541-963-3866. One of only four operating drive-in movies in Oregon. Web site: www.lagrandemovies.com.

Ladd Marsh Wildlife Area, exit 268, south of La Grande. A preservation area developed by Oregon Fish and Wildlife.

Lamb Trading Company, 203 North Main Street, Joseph. Call 541-432-5304. Native American art, books, and jewelry.

National Historic Oregon Trail Interpretive Center, 22267 Oregon Highway 86, Baker City. Call 541-523-1843. Web site: www.oregontrail .blm.gov.

Oregon Mountain Cruise Car Show, Joseph. Weekend event held each June. Web site: www.oregonmountaincruise.com.

The Potter's House, 1601 Sixth Street, La Grande. A restored Victorian home showcases the artist's Japanese-style pottery. Call 541-963-5351.

Quilts Plus, 280 South Main Street, Halfway. Call 541-742-5040. Open Mon. through Sat.; also Sun. during summer only.

Satellite Gallery, 116 Depot St, La Grande. Call 541-963-4617. Local and regional artists. Web site: www.satelliteartgallery.com.

Valley Bronze of Oregon Foundry, 307 West Alder Street, Joseph. Call 541-432-7551. Call ahead to schedule a tour. The Valley Bronze showroom is at 18 North Main Street, Joseph. Call 541-432-7445.

Wallowa County Museum, 110 South Main Street, Wallowa. Call 541-432-6095. Pioneer and Nez Perce displays and items in an old bank building. Web site: www.co.wallowa.or.us/museum.

Wallowa Lake Tramway, 59919 Wallowa Lake Highway, Joseph. Call 541-432-5331. Goes 8,150 feet up with spectacular views. Open Memorial Day through the end of Sept. Web site: www.wallowalaketramway.com.

Wallowa Land Trust, 116B South River Street, Enterprise. Call 541-426-2042. Take an expert-led hike through Wallowa's highlands. Available July through Sept. Call ahead. Web site: www.wallowalandtrust.org.

Wallowa Resources, 200 West North Street, Enterprise. Call 541-426-8053. A nonprofit group that offers day and multiday naturalist-led hikes during winter and summer months. Web site: www.wallowaresources.org.

Dining

Annie's Café, 209 Main Street, Richland. Call 541-893-6167. Very tiny and very friendly.

Blonde Strawberry, 110 East First Street, Wallowa. Call 541-886-2309. Espresso drinks and snacks.

Calderas, 300 North Lake Street, Joseph. Call 541-432-0585. Lunch and dinner Web site: www.calderasofjoseph.com.

Foley Station, 1114 Adams Avenue, La Grande. Call 541-963-7473. The best spot in town for brunch. Web site: www.foleystation.com.

Lillies of the Valley, 199 North Main, Halfway. Call 541-742-6161. Teas in the garden or cottage. Open June through Sept., Thurs. through Sat. Call for reservations. Web site: www.lillies-of-the-valley.com.

Mimi's, 241 South Main Street, Halfway. Call 541-742-4646. Cute cottagelike spot serving breakfast and lunch. Call ahead for hours.

Mt. Emily Ale House, 1202 Adams Avenue. Call 541-962-7711. Locally brewed beer with full menu. Open Tues. through Sat. Web site: www .mtemilyalehouse.com.

R&R Drive-In, 301 North Lake Street, Joseph. Call 541-432-9000. Nothing fancy, just real food with the locals.

RimRock Inn and Restaurant, 83471 Lewiston Highway. Call 541-828-7769. Dining overlooks Joseph canyon. Tepees or RV parking are available. Web site: www.rimrockrestaurant.com.

Ten Depot Street, 10 Depot Street, La Grande. Call 541-963-8766. Features local foods such as morel mushrooms from the Blue Mountains, and asparagus from Walla Walla. Web site: www.tendepotstreet.com.

Terminal Gravity Brewery, 803 School Street, Enterprise. Call 541-426-0158. Open for lunch and dinner, closed Tues. The menu includes local buffalo, and they're known for their beer. Web site: www.terminalgravity brewing.com.

Other Contacts

Base Camp Baker, Baker City's location makes it an excellent location for a vacation base camp. Web site: www.basecampbaker.com.

Eastern Oregon Visitors Association, Web site: www.eova.com.

Hells Canyon Preservation Council, La Grande. Call 541-963-3950. Find out what's being done to keep and help Hells Canyon. Web site: www.hellscanyon.org.

Hells Canyon Visitors Center, 23 miles downstream from Oxbow, where OR 86 meets Idaho border. Call 541-785-3395.

Wallowa Mountains Visitor Center, 88401 Highway 82, Enterprise. Call 541-426-5546. Open Mon. through Fri. all season; Sat., too, during summer.

Get Your Kicks on US 26

Mount Hood and into Central Oregon

Estimated length: 145 miles
Estimated time: 5 hours to 2 days

Getting There: Take US 26 from Boring, along the south side of Mount Hood and south into Central Oregon. Once in Madras, turn west on Belmont Lane. After Cove Palisades Park, travel through the town of Culver to US 97 and head south. At Redmond, go east on OR 126 to Prineville.

Highlights: Arid central Oregon is far different from soggy western Oregon. On average, there's near 300 days of sunshine. Nowhere in the state is this difference more pronounced as when US 26 descends from Mount Hood and heads toward the Warm Springs Reservation. Catch this trip on the right day, and you'll go from windshield wipers to sunglasses tout de suite. Central Oregon is a haven for outdoors lovers with rocks to rappel, whitewater to tackle, and horizons to marvel at.

From the town of Sandy, around the south side of Mount Hood, and until just before the Warm Springs Reservation, route US 26 mirrors the historical Barlow Road. Traveling down the Columbia River in the Columbia Gorge was treacherous and claimed wagons, provisions, and lives of the

Oregon's most known and recognizable natural icon, Mount Hood.

Oregon Trail pioneers. In 1845, Samuel Barlow and Joel Palmer clawed a trail around the south side of Mount Hood. Although some of the families had to abandon their wagons altogether, Barlow returned the next year, made improvements, and established the Barlow Toll Road. It took 1,800 long, hard miles for the pioneers to get to Barlow's road; they wanted to get to the fertile lands of Willamette Valley as soon and as safely as possible.

At Boring, the jokes that come to mind are numerous, but this little agricultural village is anything but dull. It all just depends on your point of view. If you garden, love someone who gardens, are interested in working blacksmiths, or just want to see something a bit out of the ordinary, stop by **Red Pig Garden Tools.** This place has everything vacation shopping should: a charming locale, good value, interesting and truly unique items, and owners, Bob and Rita, are the real deal. There's no need to be a gardener to find something good at their store. If cultivating isn't for you, consider getting something for the gardener in your life. The hand-crafted garden tools here are a true souvenir. In this two-story barn, there are more of them than anywhere in the country, over 1,000 in stock. Bob personally makes 125 different tools. Some are one-of-a-kind designs; others are modeled on vintage tools that are too cost prohibitive for the big names to produce. There are roughly 200 blacksmiths in the northwest, though only 25 are working blacksmiths like Bob. Sure, the tools are a bit more in price but talk about lasting craftsmanship. You'll replace the one you have at home dozens of times before a Red Pig one is even worn in. Ask about having your purchases shipped home to you. The barn/store is comprised of wood from two 100-year-old barns. Upstairs, classes are taught and Bob's large collection of antique tools is displayed. Nearby is the **N&N Garden Farm,** offering a bounty of herbs and heirloom vegetables. The gardens are lovely to walk around but bring closed-toe shoes. Owners Nadja and Nik also offer their artisan soaps and hand-crafted herbal gifts, such as a bug-repellent dog shampoo. Not too far away is **Starr Alpaca Farm,** where knitting and crocheting enthusiasts can pick up natural 100 percent alpaca yarn and luxurious alpaca fur teddy bears.

Five miles farther down US 26 is the town of Sandy. Continue on until the middle of town to find the **Wasson Brothers Winery** on your right, specializing in fruit wines—rhubarb, loganberry, and so on. Tours and tastings are given daily by the owners, identical twin brothers Jim and John Wasson. A bit north into town off Bluff Road is Jonsrud Lookout and outstanding views of Mount Hood. If you're in the area for the sunrise, Moth-

At Red Pig Garden Tools, novice and expert gardeners can find what they didn't even know they needed.

er Nature may present you with an astonishing photo opportunity. Just as you're leaving Sandy, you'll notice **Rainbow Creek Trout Farm.** Here you can fish without a license, bait, or tackle. They've got everything you need and are extremely family friendly. You can even have the fish cleaned (or do it yourself), then cook it on their barbecue pits.

The town of Welches has long been a draw to tourists. Shortly after the turn of the last century, Portlanders would ride for two days in a wagon to camp or stay in the hotel and attend the popular dances. At 160 rooms, **The Resort at the Mountain** may not be quaint but it is quiet, accommodating, and recently underwent an extensive updating. Extra features include yoga classes and regulation croquet and lawn bowling courts. The resort is outstandingly family friendly with a playground and volleyball court. Or you can order a picnic lunch and "hike" the surrounding area. There are two restaurants on site: fine dining at Altitude and a more casual fare at Mallards Café & Pub. Both are gracious and warm, and children are welcome. The resort also has a 27-hole golf course.

Wildwood Recreation Site might be one of the finest picnicking spots in the state; for sure, the best on this trip. The semisecluded picnic tables are available on a first-come, first-serve basis and all are located along a paved trail. But there's so much more here. The same paved trails are open to bike riding. There is a playground, a volleyball court, and horseshoe pits. The fertile Salmon River runs right through, providing excellent opportunities for fishing. Even during the summer when the river is at its lowest, it runs fast enough to fill an Olympic-size swimming pool in five minutes. In the winter, its cubic feet per second is up to 100 times faster. However, the star of the site is the **Cascade Streamwatch Trail.** The ¾-mile trail is level, paved, marked with interpretive information, and disabled accessible. The Underwater Viewing Window lets you see eye to eye with the river's inhabitants, which can include juvenile salmon and trout, crayfish, snails, and in the fall, adult Coho salmon. The Wetland Boardwalk Trail is just

See what a northwest river is all about at the Wildwood Recreation Site.

across a footbridge on the Salmon River and allows you to get up close to the wetlands without damaging the ecosystem. If you arrive in late summer, that smell is skunk cabbage and you can guess how it got its name. But it's all part of nature's greater plan.

Before the rain-sodden forest dwindles on the other side of Mount Hood, stop and enjoy **Little Zig Zag Falls.** The trail is about ½ mile, shaded, and excellent for kids. You'll follow it along next to a picture-perfect creek until you reach the 30-foot waterfall. To find the falls, turn north on FR 39, you'll see signs for the Kiwanis camp, and drive until the road ends. The petite old bridge here is from the original Mount Hood highway (circa 1920s).

Barlow Road had some dangerous spots, unkind and demanding to wagons. To view this clearly for yourself, stop at **Laurel Chute,** which was referred to as the longest hill of the entire Oregon Trail journey. Look for the signs announcing a historical marker at about milepost 50/51. At the south end of the parking lot, a short trail leads to the area. To combat the swift slope, the pioneers cut down trees and tied them to the back of their wagons, hoping to slow them down.

With regard to Oregon geology, **Mount Hood** is quite young and was still active when early settlers arrived. Volcanic flow and ash fall occurred in this area less than 200 years ago, though the major eruptions were between 1 and 10 million years earlier. This whippersnapper of a mountain is also the state's tallest, at 11,235 feet in elevation. Oregon has the longest ski season in North America and die-hards have been known to ski and snowboard here into August. But there's more at Mount Hood than just snow sports. The **Mount Hood Cultural Center and Museum** has six galleries. All focus on the fascinating history and natural history of Mount Hood and Government Camp, and even on the evolution of skiing. The museum has a fantastic program for any aspiring artist or crafter, the Arts Cabins Project, where classes are taught by local artisans in such fields as blacksmithing, bead making, watercolor painting, and much more. There are no drop-in classes; classes must be reserved in advance, so check the schedule first. A community gathering spot, the **Wy'East Book Shoppe and Gallery** is a true independent bookstore, featuring local authors along with the nationally known names. The array of subjects and styles available here cover all categories, from geology to children's to science fiction.

Timberline Lodge, an iconic lodge on an iconic mountain, is famous for so many reasons. Close to the top of Mount Hood, it's located just right

Even the drinking fountain at Timberline Lodge was created by master craftsmen.

for that stunningly long ski season. The exterior of the lodge was used in *The Shining,* a movie based on Stephen King's novel—except the film's famous hedge maze isn't here and never was. The buffet lunch is untraditional and in the best of ways: it's fresh and delicious, as well as an opportunity to eat in the lodge's stupendous dining room without a hefty price tab. The attention to detail in the décor in the rooms and suites makes guests feel as if they're staying in a vintage postcard. This isn't achieved by employing kitsch but encouraging the building's timeless beauty and classic history. If you're not staying here, that's no excuse not to stop and take in the inside and outside of the lodge. Look for the decorative rod iron. The work of the original artisans can still be seen throughout the property. Not many craftsmen can duplicate this kind of ironmongery these days. That's why the lodge's blacksmith apprenticed under the blacksmith who apprenticed under lodge's original blacksmith.

If you're eating breakfast or lunch in the Cascade Dining Room at Timberline Lodge, you can look straight down the mountain to Trillium Lake. Although the lake is pretty busy in summer months, it has an almost nostalgic feel as you sit on the dock or walk the shore. The drive to Trillium Lake is direct and easy; however, driving around the lake is not an option. From the dock is another nice view of Mount Hood, and as the mountain will be at your back from here on out, one of your last.

Welcome to the sunny side of Mount Hood. The outside temperature has most likely just changed, yet again. Enjoy the warm, dry air as you head toward the Warm Springs Indian Reservation. When you need comfort and activities but not fancy-schmancy hoopla, **Kah-Nee-Ta Resort and Casino** fits the bill. The property is comfortable for families, as you're not required to go through the casino to your room. The kids will also enjoy the natural spring–fed pools—one with two water slides There are also tennis courts, horseback rides, and tandem bike rentals. The rooms are simple and clean, and because the property stands alone, many rooms have a soothing view. The property has a lounge, two restaurants, an 18-hole golf course, and of course, a casino with slots and live games. If you'd like to enjoy a little bit of the tribe's lands, try the hiking trails that leave right from the hotel and lead to magnificent vistas. You can take one that lasts an hour or less, or get your hike on and head up 400 feet in the 3-odd miles to Raven's Roost. Two roads off US 26 lead to Kah-Nee-Ta; the first is more scenic but less direct.

The land of the Warm Springs Reservation may look tranquil, but

The road to Kah-Nee-Ta Resort on the Warm Springs Reservation

there's plenty of endorphin-rush-producing fun here. **N8TV Adventures** will pick you up at the resort and take you kayaking on Lake Simtustus, a great adventure for first-time kayakers. If you're an experienced water sports lover, then their river boarding trips have the aqua adrenaline you crave. Their whitewater rafting trip on the Deschutes River, through White Horse Rapids, is offered only by this company. All these trips are on land belonging to the Confederated Tribes of Warm Springs. For those of you who want something more cerebral in mind, the **Warm Springs Museum** will teach you about the tribes of the area, with an easy-to-navigate time-line that includes historical, economical, and cultural information. The displays are interactive with a hands-on learning approach. Lucky summer

Learn about the tribe at the excellent Warm Springs Museum.

weekend visitors are privy to demonstrations from tribal elders, such as creating with corn husks or their elaborate beading methods. The museum's building is aesthetic, very new, comfortable, and well implemented.

At the town of Madras, US 26 and US 97 intersect. To reach the following destinations, once in Madras, take SW J Street west. It will become

Belmont Lane. **Round Butte Dam** on **Lake Billy Chinook** was built in 1964 with a fish passage system that no longer allows for migration. Now a 273-foot underwater tower and a fish collection station are near completion. The tower modifies currents and temperature to attract fish, then they're sorted and trucked downstream. When they return as adults to spawn, they're once again sorted and trucked above the dam to continue on their journey. This way the salmon and steelhead runs are reestablished and the region receives power from a green source. The project has been certified by the Low Impact Hydropower Institute and is one of only 35 in the nation. Once completed, the salmon and steelhead passage will return the fish to their runs above Round Butte Dam for the first time in over 40 years. This project is sponsored in part by the Confederated Tribes of Warm Springs. The folks manning the interpretive center here provide excellent information and are very happy to answer questions. Just a bit farther is **The Cove Palisades State Park,** a busy, boat-friendly park with two campgrounds and three cabins. Along with boating and fishing, there are 14 miles of hiking trails. This park's crowd can get a bit rowdy; with 174 RV sites and 91 tent sites, it's not the best spot to go if you wish to get away from it all. From here, follow the signs to Culver and return to US 97.

About 10 miles later, you'll find **Peter Skene Ogden Scenic Wayside,** a very accommodating no-fee, day-use state park. The views of the 300-foot-deep Crooked River Canyon can be a little disconcerting for anyone bothered by heights. You've just driven across the newer bridge over Crooked River but the old bridge still exists and is for pedestrians only. There, informative kiosks and signs explain who Ogden was, a famous WWII hero from the area (the bridge is dedicated to him). All in all, it's a good spot to get your breath, stretch your legs, use the restroom, and let the dog out of the car, leashed of course.

The community of Terrebonne has an idyllic setting, like out of a classic children's novel. And to make it even more perfect, there's **Terrebonne Depot.** Located in a century-old train station that has been through award-winning renovations, the modern café has a reasonably priced menu with sandwiches, steaks, and pizzas. A patio offers a stunning view and, should the mood strike, there's a regulation-size horseshoe pit. If you prefer to eat while moving, they offer to-go items.

Smith Rock State Park, a rock climber's nirvana, is so stunning and remarkable that everyone should visit just to sit on a bench and watch the rocks change colors as the sun moves across the sky. There are four official viewpoints and each is just as well situated as the others. Three of them are simple and easy to access from the parking area. A fourth is north of the parking area and has slightly difficult trail but it isn't a long walk at all. The right lighting on Smith Rock can produce that "you gotta see this" photo to show everyone back home. If you can get here early, morning light is best. Bivouac walk-in camping is available on a bluff overlooking Smith Rock, but no RVs or fires. Care to give rock climbing a try? **Chockstone Climbing Guides** has half-day and full-day climbing classes for beginners. There's a discount for families of four or more, but kids must be ten or older to climb. Hikers will be satiated with 7 miles of trails that take in the beauty of the area without the climbing.

Just as US 26 starts to near Redmond, you'll go east on OR 126 for about 20 miles after the highway ends at Prineville. As you get close to town, the Prineville Lookout is on your left and provides a nice view of where you're headed. The largest town in the county (Crook) used to get media coverage during each presidential election. That's because from 1882

Smith Rock at midday.

to 1992, the county's vote had always been for the winning candidate. But 1996 was the year the county cast their vote for George H. W. Bush over Bill Clinton.

Throughout the state, there are hotels and motels that claim themed rooms. Perhaps it's due to high expectations for "themes," but this rarely means more than poster art, painted stencils, and a matching quilt. **Rustler's Inn** has a variety of themed rooms, all in the aforementioned manner. The rooms are clean and the property is very quiet, but the themes lack luster. At the same time, it can't be said that a theme is so overdone that a room's busy décor makes it difficult to relax. Alternatively, throughout the state are golf resorts. **Brasada Ranch** offers high-end lodging in the form of cabins or suites. The ranch has indoor and outdoor pools with lazy river and a water slide. And of course there's golf. The property is in Powell Butte on OR 126, about halfway between Redmond and Prineville.

For a small town, there are a number of excellent bronze statues scattered about. The Wildland Firefighters Memorial in Ochoco Creek Park stands for the 14 firefighters killed in Colorado in 1994; nine were from the Prineville Hotshots. It's an artistically detailed and sobering statue. In this same park is a monument dedicated to POW/MIA soldiers from WWI to present day. As you make your way through town, keep your eye out for more for more bronzes.

For some fun in the sun, **Meadow Lakes Golf** is an 18-hole course that came into existence because the city couldn't afford a water treatment facility. Thanks to irrigation and ten evaporation ponds, Prineville now has an ecological award-winning course and isn't putting anything into the Crooked River. Prineville is occasionally called the agate capital. Rock hounding is a serious and lighthearted activity here. Hard-working hounds can also unearth a thunder egg now and again. For a detailed map with instructions, information, and pictures of the best spots for unearthing a geological treasure, check with the Prineville Chamber of Commerce. A nice relaxing swim can be had at **Prineville Reservoir State Park.** Once inside the park, head toward the coves on the north shore; the trails to the water are not at all strenuous. Those who want more rustic camping should check out Jasper Point Campground, which has electricity but no showers or any designated swimming area. This is just across the water from the reservoir's wildlife area, so keep your eyes peeled and the camera ready.

Prineville is a real pioneer/cowboy/logging town, as evident by the enormous pair of bronze spurs on your left as you drive into town. At the

A. R. Bowman Memorial Museum, cowboy art and Old West artifacts are joined by pioneer items and a large collection of Oregon history books. Each spring and fall, the museum sponsors field trips to historical sites around the county. For pioneer and cowboy history buffs, this is a special opportunity, as many sites are on private land or take a guide to get to. The museum's building was originally a bank and the teller's cages are used as displays. From Memorial to Labor Day, the museum conducts biweekly tours of the Prineville Courthouse (1909), which includes getting to go up into the clock tower.

Sometimes as charming as small towns are, there's only one decent place to eat: not fine dining or fusion food, but honest-to-goodness respectable chow. Prineville has a few places where the meals are tasty, if not outstanding. **Brother's Family Diner** is exactly what the name states, a coffee shop perfect for everyone on the family. The menu isn't surprising, but at a diner it shouldn't be. It should be filled with items that are recognizable and comforting. And to top it off, the portions are more than substantial, the prices are very reasonable, and the service is down-home sweet. The servers act as if they know you, even though they've never seen you before. On the other end of town is **Toni's Bar-B-Que.** It's open seasonally and is a walk-up-and-order kind of place, and is definitely worth a swing by. When Dad cooked breakfast, it was an occasion, one that resulted in plates piled to the edge with all the delicious items no one had time to make during the week or was tired to make on most weekends. **Dad's Place** cooks their sourdough pancakes just right and the locals carry on conversations while you wait.

IN THE AREA

Accommodations

Brasada Ranch Lodging, Powell Butte. Call 1-888-701-2987. The area's high-end golf resort. Web site: www.brasada.com.

The Cabins Creekside, 25086 East Welches Road, Welches. Call 503-622-4275. Nine studio-style units with full kitchens, knotty pine décor, log furniture, and a community hot tub. Web site: www.mthoodcabins .com.

Crook County RV Park, 1040 South Main Street, Prineville. Call 1-800-609-2599. Tents, RV, and cabins. Web site: www.ccprd.org/parks_rv.cfm.

Kah-Nee-Ta Resort, Warm Springs Reservation. Call 541-553-1112 or 1-800-554-4786. A bit isolated but has something for everyone: pool with slides, casino, horseback riding, spa, and hiking trails. Tranquil views and reasonably priced rooms. Web site: www.kaneeta.com.

Prineville Reservoir State Park, 19020 SE Parkland Drive, Prineville. Call 541-447-4363. Yurts, cabins, and tepees available. Open year-round. Web site: www.oregonstateparks.org/park_34.php.

The Resort at the Mountain, 68010 East Fairway Avenue, Welches. Call 503-622-3101. Recent remodels have really bought the resort up-to-date. Web site: www.theresort.com.

Rustler's Inn, 960 NW Third Street, Prineville. Call 541-447-4185. Web site: www.rustlersinn.com.

Timberline Lodge, left on Timberline Road, Government Camp. Call 503-272-3311. Web site: www.timberlinelodge.com.

Attractions and Recreation

A. R. Bowman Memorial Museum, 246 North Main Street, Prineville. Closed the month of January. Web site: www.bowmanmuseum.org.

Andrea's Wine Shop, 67195 East Highway 26, Welches. Call 503-927-5207. Carries many Oregon wines, as well as imports. Closed Mon. and Tues. Web site: www.andreaswinegallery.com.

Chockstone Climbing Guides. Call 541-318-7170. Certified rock-climbing guides for half- and full-day classes at Smith Rock. Web site: www.chockstoneclimbing.com.

Crooked River Dinner Train. Call 541-447-5485. Features a murder mystery or robbery. Web site: www.crookedriverdinnertrain.com.

Crooked River Roundup, Prineville. Call 1-800-428-5574. June. Web site: www.crookedriverroundup.com.

Elkins Gem Stones, 972 South Main Street, Prineville. Call 541-447-5547. Owner is a third-generation rock hound and known as the local expert.

The Fly Fishing Shop, 67296 East Highway 26, Welches. Call 503-622-4607. One-day fly-fishing classes. Web site: www.flyfishusa.com.

Inga Pachukes Contemporary Gifts, 38905 Proctor Boulevard, Sandy. Call 503-826-0005. Quirky art gallery and gift store.

Maragas Winery, 15523 SW Highway 97, Culver. Call 541-546-5464. Open seasonally. Call ahead for tours, tastings, and patio hours. Web site: www.maragaswinery.com.

Meadow Lakes Golf, 300 SW Meadow Lakes Drive, Prineville. Call 541-447-7113. The course crosses the Crooked River four times and includes 10 ponds. Web site: www.meadowlakesgc.com.

N & N Gardner Farm, 9500 SE Revenue Road, Boring. Nadja and Nick. Call 503-663-0740. Open Mon., Fri. and Sun, May through July.

Pari-Mutuel Horse Races, Prineville. July. Four days of horseracing. Web site: www.crookedriverroundup.com.

Pi-Ume-Sha Treaty Days, Warm Springs Reservation. Join the Warm Springs tribe as they commemorate their treaty signing with cultural arts, dancing, and crafts. Web site: www.warmsprings.com.

Red Pig Tools, 12040 SE Revenue Road, Boring. Call 503-663-9404. Call ahead. Garden tools so good, they make you want to weed. Web site: www.redpigtools.com.

Starr Alpaca Farm, 36801 Proctor Road, Boring. Call 503-668-6998. Natural colors of alpaca yarn and teddy bears. Open most weekends, Apr. through Sept. Web site: www.starralpacafarm.com.

Wanderlust Tours. Call 1-800-962-2862. Guided canoe and kayak trips, including their special moonlight and starlight tours. Web site: www .wanderlusttours.com.

Warm Springs Museum, 2189 Highway 26, Warm Springs. Call 541-553-3331. A very well-conceived museum about the Confederated Tribes of Warm Springs from their beginnings until the present day. Web site: www.museumatwarmsprings.org.

Wasson Brothers Winery, 17020 Ruben Lane, Sandy. Call 503-668-3124. Fruit wines and gift shop well stocked for winemaking enthusiasts. Web site: www.wassonwine.com.

Wildwood Recreation Site, 65670 East Highway 26, Welches. Call 503-622-3696. Web site: www.recreation.gov.

Wy'East Book Shoppe and Gallery, 67195 Highway 26, Welches. An independent bookstore that carries big names and a lot of local ones, too.

Dining/Drinks

Brother's Family Diner, 1053 NW Madras Highway, Prineville. Call 541-447-1255. A classic coffee shop with a down-home menu.

Dad's Place, 229 North Main Street, Prineville. Call 541-447-7059. Breakfast and lunch only. Open daily.

One Street Down Café, Redmond. Call 541-647-2341. Breakfast and lunch, simple and hearty but with a northwestern flair. Web site: www .onestreetdowncafe.com.

Rendevous Grill and Tap Room, 67149 East Highway 26, Welches. The most well-known restaurant on Mount Hood has a varied menu that strives to use local ingredients.

Seventh Street Brew House, 855 SW Seventh Street, Redmond. Call 541-923-1795. Tavern features its own micro-brews, plus others. Heated deck, full menu, and families are welcome.

The Shack Restaurant & Sports Bar, 67350 East Highway 26, Welches. Call 503-622-3876. Great ambiance and food. Rain or shine, take a peek at the whimsical garden.

Terrebonne Depot, Terrebonne. Call 541-548-5030. An unusual menu for the area but done well. Outdoor dining has view of Smith Rock. Web site: www.terrebonnedepot.com.

Eat in a garden with personality at The Shack Restaurant in Welches.

Toni's Bar-B-Que, 2751 NE Third Street, Prineville. Call 503-447-1063. Open seasonally, so call ahead.

Wildwood Café on the Mountain, 65000 East Highway 26, Welches. Call 503-622-0298. Breakfast and lunch only. Open Fri. through Sun. Web site: www.wildwoodcafe.net.

Other Contacts

Central Oregon Visitors Association. Call 1-800-800-8334. Web site: www.visitcentraloregon.com.

Redmond Chamber of Commerce. Call 541-923-5191. Web site: www
.visitredmondoregon.com.

Zigzag Ranger Station, 70220 East Highway 26, Zigzag. Call 503-622-
3191. Web site: www.co.clackamas.or.us.